The Emoti

The Quest i

Sa.   _...ael son

Library of Congress Catalog Card Number: 93-83821
Publisher's Cataloging in Publication Data
Michaelson, Sandra
The Emotional Catering Service: The Quest for Emotional Independence Bibliography: p
1. Self-actualization (psychology) 2. Personal growth 3. Applied Psychology 4. Psychoanalysis

ISBN **9781520996318**
Manufactured in the United States of America
First **Prospect Books** Edition, October **1993**

- **For more of Sandra's books, visit the depth psychology website,** www.WhyWeSuffer.com

To Lyle and Hazel

Author's Note
The names and identifying details of the case histories in this book have been changed to protect confidentiality. Any resemblance to persons living or dead is purely coincidental. Anyone with a history of emotional disorders, or who feels emotionally unstable, or who is taking psychiatric medication, should not do the exercises in this book without first consulting a mental-health professional.

Contents

Chapter 1
The Six Major Features of Emotional Catering

Welcome to the Emotional Catering Service. Membership is for those who sacrifice their feelings, needs, opinions, and pleasures to serve the emotional and physical needs of others. The ECS is dedicated to the proposition that a person's worth or value in life comes from being readily available and accessible to others.

True, many of you would prefer not to be a member of this service. In ways you haven't yet figured out, you are locked into its behavioral and emotional requirements, despite the inner cry from your heart for liberation from its clutches. While you are a member, this following creed, written with intended irony, describes your psychological plight.

The Emotional Caterer's Creed:

* As emotional caterers, we agree to take responsibility and blame for other people's feelings. We allow ourselves to be put down, deprived, ignored, and pushed around to prevent the other person from having unpleasant or painful feelings. Our goal: elimination of painful or angry feelings in those around us with the intention of making them as happy and satisfied as possible. Our motto: "Our pain is their gain."

* We agree to give up pleasure and fun in life; fun is for others. We are content to let others get all the goodies and are unperturbed when nothing is left for ourselves. We believe that fun and pleasure for oneself are selfish, even greedy. We take pride in our self-denial.

* We perceive it as kindness to submit to other peoples' viewpoints and let them manage and control our lives for

us. They are always right. We agree to blind ourselves to the "negative" behavior of others and to make excuses for them so as not to disturb their inner peace.

* We agree to go through every day trying to be the perfect model of what we think others want us to be. We will concern ourselves with how other people think of us and cater to their approval even if that means giving up our own dreams and aspirations. Our lives depend on their validation and praise.

* Inwardly we believe that we are a superior race of human beings, better than the greedy, needy, cold, and demanding "takers." Unlike them, we are able to take care of ourselves without help. We do not need anything from anybody and can always work things out on our own.

* We reserve the right to identify and evaluate other people's shortcomings, but solely for the purpose of guiding others toward more responsibility and maturity. We vow to make our superior wisdom and knowledge known throughout our community, especially by providing helpful suggestions and advice. We willingly allow ourselves to be sacrificed for the "greater good" of the human race and thereby save the planet from degeneracy.

The Emotional Catering Service is a metaphor for what is commonly known as codependency. This book takes a totally new approach to codependency. It uncovers the roots of the problem, namely unresolved emotional attachments to self-denial, rejection, unworthiness, and feeling controlled. This deep knowledge from within our psyche provides the best antidote for change and growth.

This book examines the six major features of emotional catering. These features represent everyday attitudes and behavioral problems that plague many "normal" people to some degree, sabotaging prospects for health and happiness. The six features are summarized here and then examined in depth throughout the book.

Self-Denial. Why is it that we focus on what we are *not getting* rather than on appreciating what we do have? Why is it hard for us to receive positive feedback? Why do so many of us feel undeserving of what we want? It is hard for us to acknowledge the good in our lives because doing so means letting go of our self-denying victim perspective. We have built our emotional lives around the conditioned habit of self-denial.

Caterers experience discomfort in receiving. They shy away from fun and pleasure, and they deny their own feelings, thoughts, ideas, and creative talents. They are confused about their wants and needs, and believe they are not entitled to their dreams or aspirations. If they have good ideas or goals, they expect them not to work out or be well received.

Susan, a 42-year-old housewife, felt she seldom received from her husband or children the acknowledgment or consideration she said she wanted. Yet, she found it difficult to identify or express her feelings or needs. She claimed that no one would take her seriously. She lived her life according to the terms of others and set no boundaries or limits on what could be expected of her. The needs and feelings of others came first.

Susan felt uncomfortable when she received attention, praise, or recognition. She managed to sabotage experiences of pleasure or fun. It was difficult accepting gifts, favors, or emotional support. Focused more on taking care of everyone else, she worked herself to the point of ill health. Her vitality became drained and life became a major effort consisting of endless chores. Whenever help was offered, Susan replied, "No thank you, I'll be fine, really." She took pride in handling difficult situations. Wearing a cheerful mask, she made light of her emotional troubles, all the while maintaining the pain of feeling abandoned and neglected.

Fear and Avoidance of Intimacy. What is the real reason intimacy feels so threatening? This book shows how we are unconsciously drawn to those individuals who appear to give us the same hurts, neglects, and disappointments we experienced in our childhood. This subconscious willingness to repeat old patterns and experience old emotions is the real reason caterers cling to unsatisfactory relationships.

In this book, you will also learn why caterers tend to pursue individuals who are not available and how they sabotage prospects for healthy relationships.

Many caterers find themselves in relationships filled with disappointments and frustration. As a caterer, you become involved with partners who require a great deal of maintenance (ego stroking) to be happy. This sets you up for insensitive treatment, neglect, deprivation, and lack of acknowledgment. You cling to hurtful relationships in spite of the pain and take no effective action to change your circumstances. The crumbs you receive are rationalized as cake. What you perceive as love for another person is often an emotion that has more to do with dependency and fear of rejection and abandonment. In your unconscious mind, pain in relationships means love.

Caterers pursue others who are unavailable or emotionally incapable of giving. They are attracted to people they cannot have. When they do find someone who is caring and available, they soon lose interest or find him or her sexually unattractive. Caterers also have a hard time with emotional commitment because they fear losing themselves in relationships. They are convinced they will be trapped, controlled, or obligated. Closeness and intimacy are tantamount to submission, loss of control, and potential hurt.

Loaded with unrealistic expectations about relationships, caterers come to a relationship with a begging bowl, hoping the partner will fill it up with all the unconditional love, emotional nourishment, and acknowledgment they claim they did not receive from their parents.

Scott, a lawyer, had a difficult time finding the "right" woman. He ran through a series of prospects and felt unsatisfied with them all. Every time he found himself getting close to a woman, he began to see flaws in her. On one occasion, his anxious need for reassurance drove away a nice woman to whom he was very much attracted. Once he managed for a while to stay in love with a married woman who was obviously not available to him. He did on occasion date nice women, but soon found them boring and sexually unattractive.

For Scott, getting close felt like being swallowed up by the woman, a feeling he had experienced with his mother. He associated intimacy with giving up his own autonomy or losing himself in the relationship. He also expected to get stuck with the wrong woman and experience a life of disappointment, as his father had felt in his marriage.

Individuals such as Scott claim they want intimacy, yet they manage to find ways to avoid or sabotage it. Ironically, they find themselves in relationships that result in disappointment, failure, or mistreatment, continuing the same feelings and the same emotional relationship they experienced with their parents.

Obsessive Investment in the Welfare of Others.
Caretaking or catering is a psychological insurance policy against feeling controlled and abandoned by others. It is a strategy to avoid real intimacy. In this book, I teach you the concept of the *magic gesture*. This means giving to others the emotional nurturing and understanding that you feel you never received. The magic gesture is an act

of giving performed for the wrong reasons. Use of the magic gesture perpetuates feelings of disappointment and neglect. Excessive involvement in the lives of others may appear altruistic, but it really masks self-centeredness on the part of the caterer.

A caterer feels he or she can pump up a sense of value and ensure self-approval by caring for others, putting their needs first, and saving them from themselves. A caterer is like Tinkerbell in the movie *Peter Pan,* flittering around with a little wand, popping into people's lives, under the illusion of taking away their woes, and sprinkling them with happiness.

Caterers focus on another person's problems, offering suggestions and advice, getting him or her to open up while they remain closed. "Helping" another often consists of pontificating, lecturing, pointing out a person's flaws, analyzing his behavior and offering solutions. "This is what I would do if I were you," a caterer is apt to say, dropping this tidbit of advice in the plate of the sufferer. Frustration results if the person they are trying to help resists their "great" wisdom.

Jack, an energetic professional, was preoccupied with managing other people's lives. He was available to others even though it meant sacrificing his own wants and needs. He never failed to remind his wife to take her vitamins, and he showered her with self-help literature that she never read. He engaged in unnecessary self-sacrifices, lending money that was never repaid and letting strangers stay at his home. His excessive worrying and involvement with the wellbeing of others enabled him to ignore his own feelings and issues and boosted his low self-esteem.

Jack gave to others the love, attention, and approval he felt he never got as a child. Giving to others was the magic gesture that covered up his attachment to feeling emotionally deprived.

For emotional caterers such as Jack, the motivation for

helping others springs out of their own self-interest and need for approval, control, and sense of value.

Appropriate giving, in comparison, has no hidden personal agenda. There is no expectation of appreciation or reward, nor resentment if the other fails to change.

Compulsive Seeking of Approval. Why do caterers live under the microscope of other people's evaluation and judgment? What is behind the constant search to be liked and recognized? Caterers easily misinterpret and take personally other people's feelings and behaviors. For example, June, a 45-year-old teacher, felt obliged to accede to her adult nephew's request to stay with her for a few months, even though his presence would cause a disturbance in her privacy and pocketbook. Fearing the disapproval of her family, June took him in at her own expense. Behind her passivity was a paralyzing fear of disapproval.

As a caterer, your sense of value is dependent on how someone else sees you. You assume that others see you as not smart or competent enough. In your mind, you are always being scrutinized, evaluated, and judged negatively by others. You add to this deluge of external evaluation by emotionally sinking under tidal waves of self-reproach.

You may also believe that winning the "Good Housekeeping Seal of Approval" is the only way to ward off impending disapproval, shame, and humiliation. But you can't win with this approach. Striving for perfection is a method of self-torture that feeds your mind with a smorgasbord of accusations of inadequacy and failure.

To caterers, the world is judged as inferior, cold, insensitive, and withholding. Ordained evaluators, they judge others for doing it wrong or not doing it well enough. To deflect other people's gaze from their own "secret flaws," they appraise and reduce others. Unable to

11

accept themselves as they are, they live in anticipation of rejection, abandonment, disapproval, and disappointment.

Sheila, a secretary, felt the need for constant reassurance that she was liked. Her every action, decision, or expression was based on how others reacted. She tried to please everyone and to present an "all-together" image of herself. But any time she received recognition for her achievements, she felt guilty and played down her accomplishments. She saw herself as she imagined others saw her—as a loser.

Sheila's exaggerated need for approval revealed an attachment to disapproval. She sought confirmation of herself and her actions to cover up her inner conviction that she was unworthy and incompetent. Without this attachment to disapproval, she would not have felt compelled to seek so hard for approval.

The person who anticipates disapproval does not feel confident in himself and his abilities, no matter what successes he may have. Even when successful, he thinks he could have done better. A caterer anticipates failure, and consequently she does not quite manage to complete all the tasks essential to success. Rarely does she feel content with her efforts. She either blames others for her mistakes, judges others as inferior, or wallows in self-reproach.

Taking Responsibility for Others and Doing It All. Why are some people unable to delegate responsibility and feel that only they can "do it right?" Where does the expectation come from that others will fail and let you down? By doing it all and shouldering other people's burdens, we make ourselves victims of their failings and inadequacies. By doing it all, we prove how others are irresponsible, thereby creating the feelings of disappointment we are unconsciously attached to.

Caterers feel they are in control when they take over

emotional responsibility for others. Their behavior is an effort to dispel the feelings of being controlled and at the mercy of others. If a person close to them is sad, angry, or depressed, they make it their problem and might even assume they are at fault. They are often overly responsible and highly competent, and they might do twice the work without any credit or recognition.

Mary, a 35-year-old nurse, believed that if she did not take control of a situation, other people would let her down. She had little faith in others to take care of their responsibilities, and she anticipated having to come in and take over. It felt to her that others depended on her to shoulder their work. She anticipated the worst when she was not around to check on things. She felt overwhelmed by the tasks she willingly undertook. No one could do it as well as her; she "had to do it all."

In addition to shouldering other's burdens, Mary went out of her way to avoid hurting anyone's feelings. When a patient was sad or depressed, Mary blamed herself. She became apologetic and did extra work to compensate for the person's suffering. She believed she was the cause of her patients' bad moods and that she had the power to determine the outcome of their lives.

Passive Stance Toward Life. Why does a person allow herself to be controlled and directed by others and bound by their needs and demands? In this book, I examine the origin of the caterer's entrenched belief that self-autonomy and independent emotional expression mean loss of love and acceptance. I also explore the timid behavior of caterers such as Andrea, a housewife who never spoke her true feelings. An avid non-smoker, she was unable to say *No* to friends and relatives smoking in her house, and she passively endured their "lack of consideration." Andrea had learned as a child how to endure the apparent insensitivity of her parents and siblings by accommodating their needs and desires.

Caterers are adept at letting fate make decisions for them. They tend to be passive rather than initiating and to endure situations rather than make effective efforts to get what they want. They readily submit to others and fear confrontations. Unable to establish personal boundaries, they let other people define who they are and how their lives are to be lived. The result is self-denial and self-neglect.

They have difficulty speaking up for themselves, turning down things they don't really want to do, and disagreeing with another's viewpoint. Caterers also seek advice and confirmation from others, while tolerating unacceptable or abusive behaviors toward themselves.

A caterer dwells in an emotional wasteland where loved ones are lost and ambitions never materialize. Happiness is not expected. The caterer makes little effort to improve his or her situation and sometimes never entertains the notion that it is possible to alter circumstances.

These six self-defeating patterns represent a formidable barrier to the attainment of emotional independence or autonomy. Psychologist Nathaniel Branden gives this definition of autonomy:

> Autonomy pertains to a human being's capacity for independent survival, independent thinking, independent judgment; it pertains to the extent to which the source of self-approval lies within rather than without—that is, within self rather than social environment. Autonomy consists of living by one's own mind.

Take a moment to imagine what it would be like to value your own feelings, needs, and aspirations and feel good about just being yourself, without the pressure to prove your worth. Picture yourself going through your day expressing your own convictions and opinions, making your own decisions, and sharing your genuine feelings without fear or the need for approval. What would it be like to trust your perceptions and follow the inner voice of your intuition, even though to do so may go against established viewpoints?

Imagine yourself with the ability to observe objectively your feelings, motives, and behaviors without negative judgment. See yourself with the ability to admit your mistakes without fear or shame. Imagine taking full responsibility for your negative feelings or your difficult life predicaments and not putting the blame on others.

Imagine what it would be like to allow others to have their own feelings and perspectives without you feeling threatened, criticized, or needing to fix them. Picture yourself no longer needing to control, manipulate, or "repair" others to meet your own needs and desires. See yourself accepting others as they are without feeling responsible for their happiness. Imagine feeling free to express your love and caring to those close to you without the expectation of getting something back in return. Imagine feeling free to seek help from others without shame and to express your needs directly.

Sound impossible? Not at all. In the following chapters, I show you how you can attain these attributes and express your unique self without fear. The key to inner freedom is "seeing" that your present-day emotional reactions and catering behaviors are unconscious recreations of unresolved childhood hurts and grievances with parents and siblings that are transferred onto your present relationships. Current feelings are correlated with past childhood experiences, helping you to recognize your attachment to childhood feelings of emotional deprivation, criticism, rejection, and passive submission to the control of others.

Some readers may find challenging the concept that

we unconsciously hold onto childhood feelings of being deprived, rejected, and controlled. That notion is especially unpleasant to those who have been convinced they are innocent victims of someone else's negligence or malice. We want to believe that other people are responsible for our misery. But inner peace and emotional independence will elude us unless we move beyond holding parents, spouses, and society accountable for our problems and take responsibility for our own emotional complicity in our distress.

The attainment of emotional independence depends on a person's ability to overcome his attachment to being an innocent victim and learn to take responsibility for his everyday emotional reactions, his negative feelings, thoughts, and behaviors.

Unlike other books that blame adult emotional problems mostly on dysfunctional parenting, this book asserts that an individual's own perceptions and interpretations of his childhood experiences, as well as environmental influences and parental upbringing, contribute to the formation of these self-defeating catering patterns. The problem, in part, is that the child's inherent self-centered perspective has never been completely extinguished but permeates the emotional life of the adult, sabotaging relationships and success.

The final chapters provide a program of practical techniques and exercises to help the reader dismantle his catering service and establish a whole new independent orientation to life.

From my experience with my own catering patterns, I have learned that the essence of emotional independence comes in our struggle to discover the truth of ourselves, not in getting others to change. Old wounds and hurts have to be healed from within, rather than healed by someone else's love, public validation, or through the magic of some guru or healer.

Chapter 2
Caterers in Action

Emotional caterers are stuck in the following psychological predicament:

"If I go for what I want and follow my own dreams, I will offend others and pay for it in the form of disapproval, rejection, and possible banishment. I'll be seen as selfish and bad. Yet, if I go along with what others want and submit to them by giving or giving in, I'll get little in return. I will lose myself. I'll have no rights of my own. I'll be nothing and get nothing."

This no-win attitude compels a caterer to "put herself out" for others and to take responsibility for other people's distressful feelings at her own personal expense. This psychological bind corresponds to the emotional predicament she found himself in as a child with her family.

The story of Martha illustrates the struggle of an emotional caterer torn between the compulsion to serve the needs of her family versus her own needs for fulfillment and personal growth.

Martha, a 44-year-old housewife, was frantic about her twenty-year-old son who had been in and out of drug and alcohol treatment centers. Mike had twice gone off to college, but both times his parents had brought him home because of his substance abuse and failing grades. His behavior had cost Martha and her husband a lot of grief, money, and lost sleep. "How does your son's behavior make you feel?" I asked her.

"I can't tell you enough how drained and burdened I feel with my son," she explained. "I love him dearly, but there are times when I wish he'd never been born. I feel a lot of anger towards him. I also feel that if I don't rescue him or take care of him, he'll kill himself. For years now we've been bailing him out from uncomfortable situations. I really don't see how he can manage his life on his own. I fear that he'll become suicidal or self-destructive if we withdraw our emotional and financial support."

"It sounds like you live under the tyranny of your son's irrational moods," I said. "Tell me more about how it feels to be in this situation with your son."

"It makes me feel helpless and powerless. I'm so sick and tired of having to tip-toe around his moods. I'm so afraid to say anything for fear he'll explode. I just can't satisfy him. At the same time, I'm afraid I'll lose him. I also feel hurt that my feelings and needs aren't important and don't matter to him. I feel unappreciated and used."

"What do these feelings remind you of in your past?" I questioned her. "Have you experienced in your past similar feelings of being in the grip of emotional tyranny and oppression?"

"Well, my father was an alcoholic who frequently terrorized the family with his unpredictable and uncontrollable rages. My mother would respond by becoming emotionally withdrawn and depressed. She would go to bed, lock the door, and stay there for hours or days. As the oldest child, I took charge of the other children, and became the mother to create a sense of order out of the chaos of my parents' constant yelling and arguing.

"I remember occasions when Mom would disappear overnight. We didn't know where she was. I thought something terrible happened to her. I felt helpless and abandoned. I guess I numbed my feelings back then and took charge of everything, like I do today. I know I felt responsible for Mom's life, and that it was my job to keep her functioning.

"I was scared to death of my Dad. You would never

know whether or not he would be all right or in a rage. It was like walking on eggshells all the time, never knowing when the axe would fall. I had to do everything he wanted or he would hit me and hate me. I thought that if I pleased Dad, maybe then he wouldn't get so mad."

Tears began to stream down Martha's face. After a period of intense sobbing, she continued, "I was so sad and lonely as a child. I felt there wasn't anyone who cared about me or even knew I existed. My job was to take care of everybody. Who I was or what I needed didn't matter. I felt totally abandoned and cut off. I didn't realize that this hurts so deeply. I didn't even know I had these feelings."

She paused and cried some more before continuing. "You know, this is the same pain I feel about my son. It's no different. I see now that my son is both my mother and my father." Martha unconsciously transferred her feelings towards her parents onto her son. She reacted towards her son with the same expectations of loss, abandonment, and lack of recognition that she had with her parents. She did not expect him to handle his life, just as she felt her parents could not handle theirs.

"You are convinced your son would collapse if you weren't there to take responsibility and rescue him. His behavior then became a fulfillment of your expectations," I explained to her. "Your son is oppressing and controlling your life, as your father once did. You don't have a program for living without being under the tyranny of someone else's irrational behavior."

Martha listened quietly as I continued. "As a child, you took power over the control, terror, and hurt by taking responsibility for your parents' feelings, and becoming the emotional support base for them. The child part of your psyche still continues to anticipate feelings of being abandoned, disappointed, unappreciated, and hated if you do not play out this role for others. Times have changed though, and the people around you are different. On an

19

emotional level, however, those old feelings remain the same."

"It's true," Martha said, "nothing has changed. I still feel responsible for Mom's feelings today and worry obsessively about her unhappiness, trying to console her and please her so she won't get upset. She rarely listens to me. I want so much to get her to open up and see herself, so she could heal and get better. At the same time, I feel annoyed by her self-pity and hurt by her reluctance to take charge of her life."

For Martha, giving up her life for others had become a way of living. She was attached to the role of being the giver who was always available to others while getting little in return. This way of behaving was all she had ever known.

But emotional caterers have other options. A caterer can begin the process of transformation by first taking notice of circumstances where he or she does not feel entitled to receive or to get. Getting for one's self or taking care of one's self is not a sign of a greedy or selfish person. If you believe that it is wrong to take care of yourself, you will ensure that you will go through life being denied and emotionally deprived.

I suggested to Martha that she begin to observe how uncomfortable she felt in the position of receiver and how she discouraged emotional nourishment. I asked her to realize that when she was imagining being abandoned, she was the one perpetuating the feeling that no one was there for her, and that it was her unconscious or subconscious willingness to feel ignored, helpless, and insignificant that were at the roots of her pain.

Attached to Self-Denial and Self-Neglect

Caterers are almost always blind to their unconscious attachment to self-denial and self-neglect, which is the root cause of the compulsive behavior. They are convinced that this self- defeating way of reacting is the only reality, the only option. It is all they know.

They accuse themselves of being "bad" for not putting out enough effort for others, or they regard themselves as failures for not satisfying the needs of others. They shift the focus from their attachment to self-denial and helplessness (which is unconscious) onto their "selfishness" or other alleged inadequacies.

It's a vicious circle. The more inadequate the emotional caterer feels, the more she gives and the harder she tries to take care of other people's expectations. The purpose of her giving does not spring from true compassion. Instead, it is motivated by the need to ensure that others will like her and not abandon her. What the caterer believes is compassion is really her own willingness to be controlled by others and her attachment to unworthiness, helplessness, and self-denial.

The legitimate pursuit of their own real needs leaves most caterers feeling guilty or selfish. They are convinced that getting or doing what they want somehow hurts others or provokes rejection.

Meanwhile, a caterer is unconsciously drawn into relationships with individuals who are self-centered and who withhold acknowledgment of the caterer's efforts. He recreates the same hurt of being emotionally deprived that he experienced with his parents and siblings by being involved with people who are unable or unwilling to provide him with the emotional nourishment he desires.

As a caterer, the real or imagined wounded reactions of others make you feel guilty because you believe you are responsible for other people's emotional reactions, as you once felt responsible for your parents' emotional reactions. You assume the burden of responsibility for other people's lives and believe that you will be blamed and betrayed if you do not rescue others from their unhappiness. This is again a replica of your emotional experience with your parents. Having suppressed the experience of feeling emotionally exploited by your parents in childhood, you repeatedly set yourself up to be emotionally exploited in your adult years.

You justify your self-denial and attachment to being exploited with statements such as, "She will collapse without me." Or, "He'll be hurt if I don't take care of him." This belief that others will collapse or be damaged if you do not give to them serves as a rationalization to continue your secret program of being oppressed, burdened, and drained. As long as you're convinced you'll meet with disapproval and rejection if you don't make others happy, you can perpetuate inner feelings of being controlled and neglected.

Caterers cry out to themselves in frustration and resentment: "How come they are never there for me? Why is it I give others cream, but only get skim milk in return?"

But getting nothing in return is exactly the secret self-defeating game the caterer plays. This is what he is expecting and looking for, to get nothing in return for his altruistic efforts: no attention, recognition, affection, credit, acknowledgment, or appreciation. His altruistic efforts are a clever disguise for his unconscious willingness to be denied, ignored, controlled, and rejected by others.

This means that you, in adopting the catering role, set yourself up to perpetuate this state of emotional starvation and neglect. On a conscious level, however, you make others responsible for your feelings, reactions, and lack of freedom: "If only he would let me, then I could be or do what I want." Or, "If she could learn to control her anger, then I could be happy." Someone else's weakness or authority is always in the way of your happiness or serenity. Maintaining this belief means that you remain at the mercy of others who you perceive as having power and control over your life.

This unconscious emotional attachment to giving, and getting nothing in return, is deeply buried under a thick layer of protest in the form of anger, resentment, and frustration. Since expressions of anger or resentment are considered "bad form," or a cause for rejection, you coat your anger and resentment with a layer of whipped cream. On the surface, you radiate smiles of, "I'm just fine, thank you," or "I have everything under control," or "That really didn't hurt me. I can handle it." Meanwhile, you optimistically dedicate your life to new improved versions of helping, rescuing, and giving.

My Personal Experience with Catering

My own personal insights into emotional catering began ten years ago when my father entered an alcohol treatment program. Getting in touch with the effects of my dad's emotional problems on me opened up a new way of seeing myself.

After years of denial and pretense, I connected with an intense level of fury towards my father. As my blinders came off, I saw how the family had focused on my father and his emotional reactions—his anger, moodiness, and need for everyone's compliance, validation, and emotional support. Passively, we endured his vicious tirades against us, his accusations of how rotten, lazy, and no good we were. He had demanded that we drop whatever we were doing, jump into service at his every command, and never show discontent with his behavior. We never knew when his periods of relative tranquility and friendliness would give way to the raging bully.

I had lived in terror of him my whole life. The worst part was having to pretend that he was wonderful while my own feelings and opinions were stupid. During his tirades, I had often believed I was wrong and at fault. I had little choice but to mimic my mother and pretend that what was happening was really not happening. Eventually I could no longer avoid the pain of realizing that my father had no concern at all for my feelings and that he did not even care that he was hurting me.

I believed that if I protested his behavior in any way, I would be accused of being wrong and banished from his life. He always had to be right in what he believed and in what he did. Not only did the family have to accept his mistreatment, but we were obliged to like him for it as well. In my eyes, Dad was an ogre who would squash me if I did not perform or comply with his expectations. Always expecting hate and rejection, I secretly yearned for his love and approval.

It is amazing how long it took me to realize to what degree emotional support was lacking for myself and anyone else in the family. I had become accustomed to not getting any form of love, praise, acknowledgment, or sympathy. I did not even seem to know that those feelings were possible for me. I know now that I was not seen as a person in my own right. My only "value" was in serving as an instrument for the continuing satisfaction of my father's emotional desires and needs.

Having learned early to push myself and my feelings aside, I tried desperately to keep Dad happy and free from his "irrational rages" by being the "good little girl" and doing what he wanted. I discovered as an adult, after years of self-imposed martyrdom, that my life's purpose had become the maintenance of someone else's emotional stability at the expense of my own happiness. Since I spent most of my life feeling obligated to others, I did not know what it meant to have a life of my own. Without even being aware of it, I had dedicated my life to the pleasure and appeasement of others.

My hurt and fury at the circumstances of my youth were buried by an overwhelming compulsion to fix my dad's problems and then, later on, everyone else's problems. I call this reaction "the Department of Rescue Operations." As an adult, I wanted to cure him and make him the dad I had always wanted him to be. I took his resistance to change as a personal rejection of me, that he was not owning up to his problems because I was not important enough to him. I believed that his transformation was necessary for me so that I could feel recognized and acknowledged by him. If only he would change and love me the way I wanted him to, then at last I could find the love and happiness I craved. I made my emotional wellbeing dependent on his reformation.

After years of feeling responsible for his misery, I simply did not know how to stop. I kept setting myself up for more hurt. I was responding to my father in exactly the same way I had responded to him as a child. I soon learned, however, that what seemed like an altruistic act to help my father was motivated by my own self-interest.

My father's failure to change to my expectations taught me the fallacy of rescuing another person from himself. My dad's emotional problems had nothing to do with me. He was attached to his brand of misery. I believed as a child that I was the source of his unhappiness; therefore, I willingly took responsibility for "keeping him happy." I needed him to change in much the same way that he always tried to make me over to fit his idea of how I should be. By trying to take away his pain, I was being just as intrusive and controlling with him. I had needed him to be better so that I could heal the deep hurt over his lack of recognition and emotional support. Feeling controlled by him was really my problem. I could not imagine a life without my father or someone controlling me, restricting me, or holding me back.

The solution for me was shifting the focus from the behavior of my father or others to my own feelings and reactions. Despite much resistance, I finally saw how I had created, in most of my relationships, the same

25

feelings of disappointment, abandonment, and rejection I had experienced with my father. Without being aware of it, I had become attached to these particular emotions and was not willing to let go of them.

The pattern of being emotionally on-call for my family was acted out in all areas of my life. I noticed how quickly I would drop whatever I was doing to cater to the needs of others. When they needed me, I felt good and important. This pattern was so pervasive that it defined who I was, a sounding board for the problems of others.

My life was one big contest: to prove my worth in the eyes of others by being the most understanding, giving, caring, and available person around. Actually, I was trying to be everything my father was not. "You see, Dad, this is how I wanted you to treat me. If only you had been as warm and understanding as I am." In my rush to win the prize of "best human being on the planet," I blocked out feelings of love, appreciation, and contentment. I was attached to feeling not good enough, not accomplished enough.

My life seemed like an endless chore (as I had experienced it as a child). I was being controlled by this unconscious rationale: "You see, Dad, I'm doing just what you wanted me to do—work. See how hard I work and renounce myself for you." I robbed myself of the pleasure of doing what I really wanted. As an adult, when it was okay for me to be myself and honor my feelings, I resisted doing it. I was somehow determined to remain a victim of a father who would never approve of me or allow me to be myself.

In my eyes, my father did not allow me to have peace, relaxation, and the time to play. As an adult, I deprived myself of the same pleasures. Because I felt so neglected and ignored, I believed that the only way to get anything for myself was to give it to myself. In defiance, I pushed away my parents, saying to myself, "I don't need you. I can give everything I need to myself. So what if you won't show an interest in me. I can take care of myself. Who needs you anyhow."

Although this attitude led to the development of self-reliance, emotionally I set myself up to recreate the deprivation and neglect I experienced in my childhood. It was hard for me to trust that I could get anything of value from others. Consequently, I was not open to getting from others. Instead, I gave and did not get in return.

This self-sacrificing pattern had become an emotional addiction. By shifting the focus from my obsession with the behavior of others to the nature and origins of the self-denial and passivity that permeated my life, I learned that my major problem was my attachment to the hurt of being neglected and ignored. I had to accept responsibility for what little value I gave myself. I was responsible now for continuing to deny my own feelings, needs, and aspirations.

With this insight into how I maintained my childhood hurts, I stopped taking responsibility for my father's life and no longer felt intimidated by his emotional reactions. I set boundaries on his behavior in my presence and began to share with him what I was feeling about our relationship. As I focused on the origins of my feelings and detached myself from being responsible for his emotional wellbeing, we began to relate to each other in a whole new way. As I changed my perspective on him, the ogre turned into a fellow human who, throughout his life, had struggled with feeling unloved, controlled, and deprived. Like so many others, my father lived his life with the pain of never manifesting his own dreams or feeling loved or appreciated for who he was.

Chapter 3

Closing Down the Service

I have liberated myself and hundreds of others from the trap of emotional catering. If you have been running an Emotional Catering Service and want to close up shop, the secret is to learn to see yourself, others, and the world through different eyes. External improvements in your life will follow after you make this internal shift.

This shift occurs when you learn *emotionally,* not just *intellectually,* that your feelings and reactions are not caused by the words or actions of others, but by your own unconscious internal reactions to what you see, hear, and imagine.

What causes us to feel depressed, tense, or unhappy? We like to think it is the events in our lives or the behaviors of others. But a major portion of our emotional distress is a result of how we perceive, interpret, or react to circumstances, rather than what actually happens to us. It is our individual interpretation or perception of an event or situation, or even just our anticipation of some event or situation (and not necessarily the actual event itself), that's at the root of our negative feelings.

For example, if you are afraid that being yourself and being honest with how you feel will cause others to reject you, then you are responding not to an actual event but to the possibility or threat of being rejected. Being honest with your feelings may or may not result in being rejected. But your emotions, your mind, and your body are reacting as though rejection has already happened.

We can and do suffer greatly at the threat or expectation of rejection, abandonment, betrayal, criticism, or disapproval. Just the threat of being denied, refused, or made to comply to the demands of others can set off negative feelings. We inhibit ourselves and close ourselves down to avoid such occurrences. As a result, we block our own growth and creative potential.

We react to people or circumstances in our lives in negative ways because of our emotional preoccupation with being rejected, denied, deprived, or controlled. Emotionally, we are still children who see the world from the child's egocentric or self-centered perspective. Our primary concern is, "What about me?"

Most of our energy and focus is tied up in unconscious painful childhood assumptions and interpretations that are transferred onto present-day circumstances. For example, if you concluded as a child that you were treated unfairly, you will tend to perceive people responding to you unfairly in your adult life. If you felt unloved as a child, you will tend to look for evidence of being unloved in your present adult relationships.

I consider remnants of childhood egocentricity to be at the root of all emotional distress and difficulties with others. Self- centeredness or egocentricity is manifested in three major areas of emotional preoccupation: a) deprivation, b) control and helplessness, and c) rejection. These three areas represent the basic core issues of all children and are never fully extinguished in the adult.

Deprivation. We can be emotionally addicted to *not getting* what we want. We feel deprived by the imperfections of others and short-changed when we do not receive the appreciation or acknowledgment we crave. We are attracted to people or things we cannot have, thereby perpetuating inner feelings of being cheated and neglected. We anticipate being deprived, refused, and denied and often feel drained and empty. As a consequence, we are insatiable and constantly seek attention, validation, or reassurance. There's never enough love, never enough security, never enough success.

Control and Helplessness. Unconsciously, we are addicted to feeling powerless, helpless, and at the mercy of others who, from our perspective, have all the control. We feel obligated or forced to go along with another person's requests, opinions, behaviors, or mistreatment. We allow others to restrict, oppress, or dominate us, all the while blaming them for the oppression we are unconsciously willing to feel. This attachment to being compliant and powerless is disguised by our desperate attempts on the conscious level to take control of people and events in our lives.

Rejection. We anticipate being hurt and betrayed. We hold onto grudges and hurts and collect them in a special grievance file in some area of our mind. We are convinced that if we express who we really are and what we really feel, we will be rejected or disapproved of. This belief gives us a great excuse to remain controlled and dominated.

We spend much of our lives watching ourselves being observed by others. Inwardly we feel like hamburger in a meat market: nothing special. We do not expect others to take us seriously. To fulfill our inner prophecies of being hurt, we often subconsciously choose others who will hurt us or treat us with insensitivity. Shame hangs over us like a dark cloud. To forestall the betrayal and abandonment we are sure will happen, we make ourselves indispensable to others and present an image of perfection.

We would like to believe that these feelings are caused by situations or people outside of ourselves. We want to see ourselves as innocent victims of other people's mistreatment and automatically assume that others deliberately ignore, hurt, insult, or deprive us. We want to believe that all we need to do is change the outer circumstances (partner, job, or residence), and our negative feelings will go away. This is why we feel compelled to fix things or somehow make others the way they are "supposed" to be.

But trying to change others to rid yourself of your own emotional reactions only leads to more frustration and dissatisfaction. It is very seductive to believe that: "I'll feel good if I can just get him or her to change or leave me alone. Or if only I could find the right person, or find the right career, I'll be happy. Or if I just sacrifice and give enough, some day they will acknowledge me. Or I'll be happy if I could only win the lottery." You make yourself even more dependent on situations out of your control when you focus on outer circumstances or others as the cause of your emotional distress.

Often people ask me, "What do I need to do? Just tell me what actions I need to take to make my life more creative and productive?" It is not so much what you do but how you feel about what you do. You need to ask yourself, "Why do I overeat? Why do I need my partner to change? Why do I feel inadequate? Why do I always expect the worst? Why am I feeling down today?"

All your behaviors and reactions are motivated or prompted by feelings. These feelings need to be acknowledged and understood. You need to examine how and why you perceive events or people the way you do and understand the motives behind your actions. Appropriate actions or behavior automatically follow true insight into your feelings or interpretations of reality.

Caterers search for the "magic pill," the right words, the right book, or the right healer to make their pain go away. They are eternally waiting for someone or something outside of themselves to confirm their worth or importance. They are reluctant to look at why the pain is there and where it comes from.

I have found in myself and others a resistance to change, even when we know the old feelings and behaviors are not in our self-interest. We tend to feel (as we did in childhood) that we have no control over our emotional reactions or our circumstances. Repeatedly, I see people avoiding positive steps to overcome their distressful situations while recreating the predicaments that make them so miserable, such as in the following examples.

Marsha knew that being involved with a married man would most likely end up in hurt, rejection, and abandonment. Her affair took up a lot of time and energy that could have been spent looking for an available partner. Yet, she felt emotionally "possessed" by the situation and could not end the affair. Periodically, she would endure strong episodes of hurt, abandonment and loss—feelings to which she was unconsciously addicted. The affair served as an opportunity to experience again the same painful neglect and unavailability she experienced with her father in childhood.

Mark knew his life was out of balance. He spent more than seventy hours a week at his career. To relieve the stress, he drank too much, and he became physically exhausted and unable to sleep. In spite of the knowledge that his health was being endangered and his family was feeling alienated by his compulsion to work, he just could not let up. "I can't stop," he stated. "If I stop, I wouldn't know what to do with myself. I know this is killing me, but I have to do it."

Many people settle for bad health, unhappiness, struggle, failure, and disappointment as if no other options were available. I have even seen people give in to a fear of growing stronger and more successful. That happens when they leave a relationship, or even their therapy, just as positive changes start to take place.

Change is difficult for us because it represents the attempt to go beyond or defy the internal restraints and prohibitions that we still carry from childhood. Some of us perceived that we were not supposed to be too good; thus, we limit our own potential. Many of us were conditioned in childhood to blind ourselves to the negative in our parents or in how our family conducted itself. Just as our parents resisted facing themselves, we now resist facing ourselves and our participation in the tragedies of our lives.

All growth, physical and emotional, involves separation. We separate from the womb, from our family, from school, and from each level of psychological growth. Separation implies "dying" to the old way and giving birth to the new. This process of death-rebirth is accompanied by feelings of vulnerability. That is one reason why we have an instinctive fear of change. It does not feel safe. We associate inner growth with giving up something to which we are attached. This growth feels more like loss or annihilation rather than gain or new life.

On an emotional level, we are still childish, and we often react like children. The logical, rational mind may have little power over this emotional side of us. Most people are unaware of how this child-consciousness runs their emotional life. Many of our emotional reactions are replays of our reactions as children. In other words, our feelings and reactions as adults may have more to do with childhood hurts, misinterpretations, and unresolved issues than with present reality.

This child-consciousness that lies beneath our adult awareness remains steeped in infantile expectations and threats, such as the desire to be served on demand or the threat of disapproval (see Appendix E for more on how the child perceives reality). This child part of our psyche is also bound by the commands and restraints the child heard from parents.

An individual recreates familiar childhood emotional experiences in the dramas of her present life. Her spouse becomes a resurrected mother, father, brother, or sister

33

who, as she perceives it, mistreated or abandoned her. Unconsciously we expect to be treated by others in our adult life in the same way we felt treated by our childhood family, thereby repeating the life we thought we had escaped.

We also treat ourselves in the manner we felt treated by our parents and siblings. For example, if you felt your parents discounted your creative talents, you are likely to discount your abilities. If you believed your parents did not regard you as important, you will likely not value yourself.

We repeat self-defeating patterns as if our minds are stuck in a groove. We use present experiences to play off old feelings and expectations. Our brains have trouble differentiating between reality and what we believe is occurring. Whether an event is real or imagined, we respond emotionally in the same way.

Here is an everyday example of how a person transfers the past onto the present. Maria asked her husband Tom what his plans were for the coming Saturday. Tom told her he had to go to the office to finish some work. Maria became very upset and scolded him for not advising her sooner about his plans. "You never let me in on what you're doing," Maria complained, feeling disappointed and depressed.

In a session, Maria described to me her feelings when Tom told her he had to work. She felt powerless, unloved, abandoned, and disappointed. She traced those feelings back to her father who worked compulsively. As a child, she looked forward to spending time with him on weekends. But her father invariably went to work, leaving her feeling ignored, abandoned, and disappointed. She felt she had no choice but to endure his absences.

Maria realized that she was transferring onto Tom her old feelings from childhood. She felt her father had never let her into his life. She used the reality of Tom's going to work on Saturday as an opportunity to reel off those familiar childhood feelings of being rejected and unimportant.

Maria had insisted on blaming Tom for her feelings, only to perpetuate her willingness to indulge in the hurt of her past wounds. She looked for hurt, neglect, and rejection because she was attached to those feelings and because she did not know how to operate outside of those old expectations.

The unconscious need to re-enact old hurts takes precedence over will power. We identify ourselves with the old wounds and emotional conflicts from our past. Feeding these conflicts keeps us intact. We do not know ourselves without fear, without conflict, or impending crisis. For many of us, the depths of pain and sacrifice give us a sense of who we are.

We use pain as a way of bonding with others. We feel our existence through our own suffering and through the suffering of others. Life is associated with pain, and pain is preferable to being alone. As one client expressed it, "Somehow, I feel that if I become happy and successful, I'll die. I cannot quite believe that life can be a happy, joyous experience."

The ability to see and understand how you compulsively repeat past feelings and behaviors gives you the opportunity to make conscious choices about your present actions. It enables you to understand the motives behind your behaviors and helps you to face your fear of change.

Fear of change keeps us from becoming emotionally free. We fear our own existence, our own individuality. Why is this? Take a moment and reflect on the following question. "If I could allow myself to be open and honest with my feelings, perceptions, and aspirations, what do I feel would happen?" Here are some common responses to this question.

- I won't be loved. I'll be ostracized, condemned. I won't be accepted, I'll be alienated from others.
- It will result in confrontations with others, and I will be disapproved of.
- I'll have to be responsible for my life, my own decisions and actions, and have to rely on my own judgment. I'll have no one to blame but myself for how my life turns out.
- It's bad to be somebody special. I would be set apart from the rest and not liked.
- Others would be hurt.
- I would be alone, abandoned, cut off from others. I would feel separate from everyone.
- The more I feel my worth, the more there is to lose. I could get hurt and feel loss. If I do not live fully, I cannot die, for I am already dead to myself.

You can see from these responses that it takes great courage to value oneself and take responsibility for one's life. But are these fears real or just imaginary threats? Could we be using these fears to justify our attachment to our familiar emotional prison?

A New Approach to Recovery and Transformation

My approach to transform emotional catering into emotional independence involves a change in the way we see ourselves and others. As I've said, change happens when we understand that our emotions are caused not by others, but by our interpretation of how we perceive external forces acting upon us. In most cases, we misinterpret what we see because we have a secret investment in feeling deprived, controlled, rejected, criticized, or wronged in some manner. We ourselves keep open the inner doorways to feeling abused, hurt, and denied. Even though others may indeed be hurting or controlling us, we are still responsible for how we choose to react to their behavior and how we let it affect us. Talking, thinking, intellectualizing, and hoping for happiness only work at the surface of awareness. Nor does permanent growth occur with other common approaches, such as positive affirmations, letting God handle it, surrogate parenting, or the "just-do-it" philosophies. These methods do not penetrate the unconscious assumptions or beliefs to which we are attached. Consequently, they rarely result in any permanent lasting change.

Since we have to work so hard to love ourselves and to let go of negative emotions, some part of ourselves is obviously holding onto the negative and resisting change. If loving yourself or letting go of negative emotions were an effortless natural process, there would be no resistance to letting go of negative beliefs and feelings.

Trying to block out negative thoughts with techniques such as positive affirmations is just another way of paying attention to them. The more a person tries to make his emotional conflicts disappear without understanding how he is attached to them, the more conflict he creates in himself.

At an unconscious level, you are choosing to indulge in the distressful negative feelings that you are experiencing, although on the surface you protest against them. Life is based on interaction, not cause and effect. You interact with life and co- create your present circumstances. You participate in the emotional dramas of your life. If you feel you are in a bad marriage or a dead-end job, you need to look at your emotional participation in choosing those situations and in maintaining them. Your actions speak louder than your complaints.

Take a moment to reflect on how it would feel to be told that you are responsible for everything that has happened in your life, that no one is to blame for the negative feelings that you experience, and that you are responsible for the choices you make and the people you are with.

This reluctance to point the finger at ourselves stems from shame and the feeling of being diminished. We feel reduced when we realize that we create and maintain most of our mental and emotional problems. The need to blame others and to validate our right to suffer are attempts to avoid feeling guilty about our own passivity. To take responsibility for our pain, our emotional reactions, and our passivity often feels very uncomfortable.

No one can deny that life is filled with unfairness and that cruel people exist. The emotionally independent person, however, accepts this reality and refrains from taking personal offense to people or events. She has relinquished her childish self-centeredness, and that gives her the ability to face herself, her behavior and her feelings without shame. Such a person has the capacity to be objective, to see other people's behavior, feelings, and motives independent of her own fears and needs. She doesn't need others to be just like her or to see things her way. Caterers, on the other hand, easily judge and evaluate others and assume they have the correct perspectives about the motives and behaviors of others.

Emotional independence has nothing to do with self-centeredness, selfishness, or narcissism. It has nothing to do with isolation from others, the ability to live alone, or the feeling of not needing others. It means much more than the ability to hold down a job and take care of yourself or your family financially.

Emotional independence means that, because you are no longer tangled up in your own desires, pains, and preoccupations, you are able to be present to those around you. Because you are no longer focused on "needing" validation from others, you are able to give of yourself freely. You give because you choose to give, not because you feel obliged to give. Freed from the pressure to give, you tend to give more. Consequently, you develop more compassion for others, rather than less.

As an emotionally independent person, success is based on "experiencing" yourself and your life rather than based on acquiring possessions, security, approval, or recognition. You exude an inner confidence, a certainty about yourself that comes from within, that is not dependent on your performance or on approval from others.

When you no longer strive to become worthy in the eyes of others, you can simply be yourself. Once you are true to yourself, everyone around you responds more positively. A natural balance unfolds between taking care of yourself and caring for others. Only when you are yourself without needing approval or fearing abandonment can you be truly compassionate and serving to others.

The coming chapters explore case histories and examples of our emotional addictions to being deprived, controlled, and rejected and how our addictions to these feelings show up in our everyday lives.

Chapter 4
Pursuit of the Elusive Cookie

More "principles," ironically presented, from the ECS Creed:

- Never be happy or satisfied with what you have. Get into the feeling of being short-changed and treated unfairly. Notice how others want to deny and refuse you.
- Focus resentfully on others who "get," while you are deprived and go without.
- When gains materialize, shift your focus to what is missing and not working out for you. Go after what is hard to get. Whatever is easily available is dull and valueless.

While these principles defy common sense, they are characteristic of the self-denial and the "never enough" attitude that make up emotional catering. An American Indian fable exemplifies the caterer's underlying attachment to self-denial and feelings of never being satisfied. I have updated it to fit our time and circumstances.

A happily married couple were raising twin sons. The boys displayed entirely opposite personalities. One twin was negative and pessimistic in his attitude toward life, and the other
was extremely positive and optimistic.

The negative twin complained about everything. Nothing satisfied him. No matter what was given to him, it was never enough. He continually grumbled and complained about all the injustices he felt he was forced to endure. He felt criticized and rejected when his parents tried to give him helpful suggestions and claimed that no one loved him enough. Meanwhile, he believed that his brother got all the benefits.

By comparison, the positive twin was pleasant to be around. He accepted everything without complaint and did what he was told. He expected that everything would work out for the best and would only express kind thoughts about everyone. He put others first and never acted selfish or demanding. No matter what awful thing might befall him, he would smile and say, "It's alright, I'm fine."

The parents worried that both boys were unbalanced in their outlooks. The negative or pessimistic twin seemed destined to be perpetually dissatisfied, while the positive or optimistic twin was a sitting duck for others to take advantage of. The parents pondered how to help the two boys become balanced, and soon they came up with a plan. They decided that, as expensive as it would be, they would buy the negative twin everything he conceivably wanted in hope of finally satisfying him. While the boys were at school, they went shopping and filled the negative twin's room with dozens of gifts.

To balance the positive twin, they dumped a load of horse manure on his bedroom floor. Surely the injustice and cruelty of such treatment would shake this twin out of his Pollyanna stupor and make him see that life was not always as rosy as he wanted it to be.

When the boys came home, the negative twin went to his room with the usual frown on his face, and immediately exclaimed in disgust: "What a mess. Who did this? I don't want the stereo over there. And why did you get me those video games? You know I hate them. What am I supposed to do with all this stuff? This is a cheap T.V. I want a large wall screen one." And so, he was even more miserable than ever.

The positive twin happily skipped into his room. A

moment later he came running out, shouting in excitement, "Mom, Dad, do you know where there's a shovel."

"Why do you want a shovel?" they asked.

"Well, there's a big pile of horse shit on my bedroom floor and I just know that if I dig deep enough there must be a real horse underneath."

Most emotional caterers immediately identify with the positive twin and fail to recognize the negative twin within themselves. The positive twin becomes a cover for the underlying dissatisfaction of the negative twin. Outer abundance does not necessarily result in contentment or satisfaction. Both twins represent the inability to feel the benefits of life: the negative twin feels he never gets enough; the positive twin constantly denies himself.

Caterers also represent the inability to receive, whether that be attention, recognition, love, or the right partner or the right job. When something is denied them, they want it even more. They are addicted to squeezing juice out of a dried-up fruit, expending their efforts to get nothing in return. Here are some real-life examples.

Linda and Matt took their six-year-old son Jake out for a day of fun that included miniature golf, a movie, and restaurant. Linda ordered Jake his usual five-pack of chicken nuggets. When Jake realized he was getting only five nuggets, he screamed in protest, "I wanted nine pieces, not five." He was inconsolable.

Linda calmly replied, "Well Jake, why don't you eat the five and if you want more, we will order some more."

"No," he screamed, "I want nine nuggets and I want them now."

"Jake, this is how it is, eat the five nuggets and we'll see." But he refused to accept this compromise. "O.K. then, I won't eat anything," he insisted.

Indeed, he went without food that evening, not wanting to let go of the feeling of being denied and refused his nine nuggets. His parents were perplexed. "We spent the entire day doing things that he wanted to do," Linda said, "and then he goes berserk over a few nuggets."

A similar episode occurred in another family. Harry waited an hour for his wife to come home and fix dinner. He was hungry and annoyed. When Cindy arrived home, she did not feel well and wanted to relax.

"But what about my supper?" Harry exclaimed. "I'm sorry, dear," she said, "but I just don't have any energy to make anything for you. I had to work overtime and I have a bad headache. There are some leftovers in the frig if you want to heat them up."

Harry fumed to himself. "She gives all her energy to her work, and none to me. Now I have to go without my dinner." He chose not to heat up the leftovers. Instead he starved and deprived himself of food that evening, making himself more the victim of his wife, who he perceived as refusing and denying him his basic right to be fed.

Our lives are filled with similar episodes of feeling denied, refused, starved out, deprived, and short-changed. Many of us are convinced we are not supposed to get what we want in life. Nothing is ever enough for us right now. We are always hungering after something else—another partner, more money, more recognition, fancy furniture, passionate sex, more support, or more wholeness. When was the last time you ever felt thoroughly satisfied with yourself and everything in your life? How long did that feeling last?

We blame others or the outside world for our inner dissatisfaction and expect someone else or something else to satisfy our inner cravings for unconditional love and the immediate gratification of our wishes. We doom ourselves to a life of emotional deprivation, always recreating the feeling of missing out on what could have been. Yet we find subtle innovative ways to sabotage getting what we

43

want and find justifications for not taking the necessary steps to realize our dreams. We look for disappointments in our relationships, our jobs, and our children. We feel let down by life.

We never imagine that the source of our *never enough* problem is an unconscious attachment to the feeling of *not getting,* even though we appear to be striving hard to get. "Getting" feels forever out of reach or, when it does materialize, uninteresting. We are entangled in a "crumb" mentality. No matter how much pleasure or satisfaction we get, we want more or something else and feel in the grips of an insatiable inner hunger. Some of us only feel "normal" when involved in some kind of struggle or challenge.

Joe, a 50-year-old businessman, was seldom content with his accomplishments. He had several successful businesses, but found himself bored when he attained the success he wanted with a new business. He felt good only when starting up a new business.

Joe remembered when, as a youngster, he pleaded and begged his mother for a bicycle. She told him she could not afford one. He sulked but persevered in his attempts to get his mother to purchase the bicycle. When he finally got it, the bike sat unused in the garage after a few weeks of use.

Joe was hooked on the struggle to get, but was not interested in, or could not assimilate, the attainment of what he said he wanted. As he put it, "If I felt I had everything I wanted, then I would feel no reason to live. Life would have no meaning or purpose. I feel more of a thrill trying to achieve some goal, than actually reaching the goal."

Many people spend their lives being unhappy because they do not have some desired object or person (a new car, house, boat, better job, more responsive spouse). But as soon as they get what they want, they shift focus onto something else and keep the misery going. They convince themselves that if they obtain what they want, they will never be unhappy again.

Notice how you may suffer if, for example, you are not able to buy a new car (or whatever it is that you want). You think you want a new car, but your sense of anxiety or urgency for a car indicates an unconscious willingness to indulge in feeling deprived of it.

Spinning Your Wheels to Get Nowhere

Caterers dedicate their lives to the pursuit of "getting nowhere." Like a hamster on a spinning wheel, they expend time and energy getting nowhere and ending up with nothing. That is because they really do not expect to get recognition, praise, financial rewards, and so on.

Claire, a secretary, played out the role of professional saboteur in her life as she repeatedly walked away from lucrative career opportunities. Just when she started to move up in her career, she quit and did something else. She rationalized this pattern of job-hopping by telling herself that she wanted more adventure in her life. She even walked away from her husband when things got better in their relationship. The result was that, at 52, she had nothing except regret over missed opportunities. She felt depressed because her present job was not challenging enough. This woman sabotaged positive opportunities in her life because she was unconsciously addicted to spinning her wheels.

Ellis, a banker, wanted to be a writer. But despite all the time and energy he put into writing, he was unsuccessful. He noted that working hard and getting nowhere was a pattern in his life. Ellis had twice married women he claimed were cold and withholding. He tried hard to get warmth, attention, and interest from them. Again, success eluded him. He was unconsciously addicted to the "empty breast." He would pick people or set up

45

situations in which he would waste his efforts squeezing out dribbles of satisfaction. His attempts to get juice out of a dried-up fruit masked his attachment to the feeling of perpetual disappointment.

Like the negative twin in the Native American fable, we look around for ways to be deprived, even though we have more than enough. In some cases, the more we get, the more dissatisfied we become. Or, like the positive twin, we manage to lose or give away what we have, all for the unconscious purpose of retreating back to our familiar sense of not having enough. We have become unconsciously attached to the feeling of being refused, denied, and not getting what we want. Here are some more manifestations of this hidden attachment.

The Bag Lady Syndrome

Jane had an emotional preoccupation with feeling that "I'm going to end up as a bag lady combing the gutters for food." Every tax season she encountered this fear of starving in the gutter. Jane felt that "they take everything from me. I'm not supposed to have anything. Nobody gives a hoot what happens to me." She complained about how little she had compared to her wealthy neighbors and about the high prices she had to pay for things. Her husband, she said, never made enough for her to feel secure.

Yet Jane had a spending problem and managed to blow money on clothes, restaurants, vacations, and new furniture. She seemed determined to keep her rendezvous with the gutter. She did nothing to increase the family income in order to feel more secure about retirement. Instead, she blamed her poverty mentality on the government, which robbed her of her goodies, and on her husband who, as she saw it, did not provide for her properly.

Jane was unable to feel satisfied with what she had.

Whatever her situation, it was never enough. She had grown up in a poor family and felt denied the things others kids had at school. As a child, she had felt she was always on the verge of starvation. Her fascination with the gutter was a continuation of her childhood anticipation of impending doom and deprivation, as well as a way to perpetuate herself as a victim of others who she saw as refusing to "give" to her emotional or physical nourishment.

Worst-case scenarios such as the "Bag Lady Syndrome" indicate our unconscious attraction to loss and *not getting* what we want. We can use our imagination to spin off catastrophes that never occur. We react to these imaginary tragedies with physical stress and emotional anxiety, as though they were real and present in the moment.

Marcy fumed for days as she quietly went about making preparations for a party. She felt her husband would say *No* if she asked for his help. So she planned to do it all herself, yet still resented him for his lack of consideration. When Marcy did ask her husband to run a few errands, she got what she expected. He replied, "I'm sorry honey, but I have to finish the patio for Lucille (his sister). I promised her I'd have it done today."

"You always have time for her, don't you? Never for me. I guess I'm at the bottom of the totem pole," Marcy protested. "You never go out of your way to help me or give to me. I never get enough attention from you. What I do is just not important to you, is it?" For days, she held onto the injustice of "he's always giving to others, but not to me," and retaliated by refusing to do his laundry for two weeks.

Life gives us plenty of opportunities to feel refused and denied. Every time a child hears the word *No* from his parents, he can feel denied and refused. Siblings also can be great sources of deprivation. Jenny always complained that Bill, her brother, got more privileges than she did. In her eyes, Bill was favored and got everything he wanted. The more she saw Bill get, the more Jenny felt denied and refused. Interestingly enough, Bill saw Jenny as getting more than he did. He saw her as the favored child and seethed with the injustice of it all. Many children grow up perceiving the parents as "great deprivers." They then transfer their expectation to be deprived onto their adult relationships.

Every time Lois denied sex to Tim, he would sulk. According to Lois, "Tim has an insatiable sexual appetite. If he had it his way, we'd be doing it every day of the week. I love Tim and love sex with him but I just can't handle it every day. He always seems to hit on me when I'm tired or when he knows I'm not in the mood." Emotionally, Tim fed off the feeling of being refused by Lois.

One problem dieters have with diets is the feeling of being denied what they really want to eat. Most dieters will dwell constantly on the foods they cannot have or mourn for the quantity of food they used to eat, indulging all the while in feelings of being starved out and deprived. People who have problems with alcohol can also feel deprived and denied of their source of "satisfaction" when family members insist on "robbing" them of their pleasure.

Sam, a 44-year-old store owner, felt denied and deprived by his wife's reluctance to invest in the stock market. He felt she was denying him an opportunity to make the score of his life. However, after several large loses on Sam's stock picks, his wife had concluded that he was more interested in experiencing loss than in making good investments.

Take a moment and think about times in the past week you might have felt deprived or refused. Write down childhood experiences of the ways you felt denied or deprived by your parents or siblings. Notice how your life is permeated with the underlying discomfort of being disappointed and denied.

Settling for Less

Rhonda, a writer, dreamed she was at a banquet. She noticed that the food, though abundant, was unappetizing, and she left the banquet feeling dissatisfied. The banquet in her dream was a metaphor for how she was experiencing her life. She always felt she missed the good stuff and settled for less. Her writing, for instance, never really attained the success and recognition she wanted. Her husband was not "ambitious enough" in her eyes. She could not afford the house she really wanted and had to settle for an inferior car. For Rhonda, life meant settling for less and missing out on what she really wanted.

Another way to settle for less is to sacrifice your aspirations so that other people are fulfilled. Janie, a sculptor, related how as a child she would give up her supper and go hungry so that her corpulent father would be able to eat his fill. If the father did not feel satisfied, even her mother would offer up her food and go without. This form of sacrifice later became a pattern in her relationships. She would willingly give up her time, energy, and interests to others, at a great cost to herself.

Another way to feel denied is to spin out fantasies or daydreams related to refusal and deprivation. Matthew, a 30-year-old builder and married man, developed a strong attraction to another woman. He spent a lot of time fantasizing how wonderful sex would be with this woman. The more he thought about her, the more dissatisfied he became with his wife. His wife, he felt, did not give him the passion, the excitement, the thrill he got when he was near the other woman. He knew he would not leave his wife and children, so he satisfied himself with a fantasy of

49

passion and love that would never materialize.

Many of us spend much time indulging in similar forms of romantic fantasies, or on reflecting what we would do if we won the lottery. As we get older, we fear that it will be too late to realize our dreams, and we dwell on our "missed out" opportunities. Motivated by fear of what will or will not happen, we torture ourselves with feelings of never getting what we want.

The world is unfair, and there will always be others who appear to have more or be happier than us. We can use this fact to foster feelings of being deprived, cheated, and victimized.

Watching Others Get

Beth Ann, a secretary, made a second career of peeping (looking visually for ways to feel deprived, neglected, or criticized) at the bounty possessed by others. Unmarried, with no children, she felt life was passing her by, and that she would be left out at the banquet of life. She felt jealous of friends who had fallen in love. She felt envious of a coworker who had bought a new house. And then there was her friend Nell who just had a new baby.

Beth Ann complained that those around her appeared to get it all without effort. Targets of her negative judgments were wives of wealthy husbands, winners of state lotteries, business colleagues more successful than herself, and athletes and entertainers with enormous incomes. The more she belittled them for coldness, selfishness, blind luck, and lack of character, the more she secretly relished her own taste for deprivation and the unfairness of their good fortune. She would claim to herself, "At least I work hard and earn whatever I get." Her superior attitude was a defense to save face and to mask her inner propensity to indulge in feeling gypped, deprived, and taken advantage of.

"Why is it that everyone else gets, but not me?" she moaned. "I spend most of my time comparing myself and what I have to what everyone else has. I always come up short. What's wrong with me?"

Beth Ann's frustration, even bitterness, about feeling short-changed had the effect of impeding her progress in getting what she wanted. Focused on what she did not have, she could not see how she sabotaged her relationships with men or chose to stay in a dead-end job with no prospects of advancement.

Many individuals with an addiction to self-denial grow up perceiving that to get what they want, they have to work hard and struggle. Brett, a health worker, related several incidents that illustrate this belief.

"I remember that if I wanted to go out and play with friends, I would have to earn this privilege by doing dishes, cleaning out the garage, and other chores and errands. To get what I wanted, I had to beg or work hard for it. I also had to do it right or in a certain way. If I did not perform according to their expectations, my parents would withhold from me and not give. I grew up believing that I could only feel fulfilled as long as I worked hard and someone gave me permission," he related.

Brett believed that getting in life depended on how much others were pleased with him, and that he got only what was allowed or deemed by others. A pay raise depended upon his ability to conform and perform to the boss's expectations, just as childhood privileges came from doing his chores according to his parents' expectations. Because of this belief, Brett adopted a passive stance with others. It was hard for him to accept the notion that he could "get" what he wanted without another's permission or without a painful struggle.

If I Get What I Want, Others Will be Deprived

Jill, a housewife, wanted to go back to college but

could not bring herself to do it. She claimed her children and husband would suffer from her absence and inattention. She felt she had no choice but to give up her personal goals and sacrifice herself in order to serve her family. Jill was convinced that "to get what I want will deprive others or hurt them in some way. If I get, the other person loses." This belief is a potent way to remain stuck in the mire of *not getting* for oneself.

An individual can disguise his own fears of success, as well as his attachment to refusal and deprival, by claiming that others will be hurt by his success or fulfillment. He can feel considerable guilt for allegedly depriving others if he does what is best for him. This guilt for allegedly letting other people down serves as a rationalization for the person's own unconscious willingness to feel deprived or denied.

Guilt also indicates an unconscious identification with the person you perceive as feeling deprived and cheated. The guilt brings to mind your own experience of feeling deprived and cheated by what appeared to be the selfishness of your parents and siblings. However, you feel the guilt because you yourself are sneaking in the feeling of being refused or deprived. To cover up this emotional attachment, a psychological defense is produced: "You see, Mom and Dad, how I never let other people down. I am ready to give up what I want to be available to them. Unlike you, who always put your interests before me." This is the magic gesture defense.

Guilt, in this case, masks the caterer's hidden attachment to feeling let down and disappointed by other people's self-indulgence. Sometimes this inner attachment is side-stepped by focusing instead on being the aggressor, the one who lets others down, instead of the one who is being let down. As a person understands his own sensitivity to being let down and disappointed by the self-interests of others, the guilt of hurting or depriving others dissipates. Guilt and fear are the major negative emotions that justify a person's passivity and ensure that he or she will continue to feel deprived and dissatisfied.

The notion that if one gets, then other people will be deprived goes back to childhood feelings with parents and siblings. Lynn, a receptionist, grew up believing that if she went out and had fun with her friends, her mother would become depressed and unhappy. Lynn explained, "Mom always wanted me to be around and available to her. She looked so sad when I wanted to play with my friends. Many times, I would stay home just to keep her company when I could have gone out with my friends." Lynn deprived herself to keep her mother happy, a pattern she later continued to express in relationships.

Another client, May, remarked that whenever she won at table games with her father, he would sulk and look hurt. She took responsibility for her father's bad feelings by believing that her winning caused her father to feel bad. She grew up with a built-in resistance to winning and success. May chose to deny herself the benefits of getting for herself rather than risk a negative emotional reaction from another person.

Cloaked behind the outer facade of "virtuous sacrifice" is the attachment to being deprived and denied. Some caterers practice a kind of compulsive goodness. In fact, compulsive goodness is a kind of trademark of emotional caterers. They love spending money on other people, for instance, but cannot give to themselves. "Oh, that's all right, I don't need anything," they stoically remark. They will easily give to other people, churches, organizations, and so on, but have great resistance in giving to themselves.

Caterers assume that wanting to receive is an indication of greediness. "If I express my feelings and needs and pursue what I want, I'll be regarded as a withholding, selfish person. Mom and Dad taught me that, and besides religion also says that getting for yourself is bad." Caterers often believe the worse possible accusation is to be called selfish or greedy. For a caterer, being selfish means being seen as inadequate, inferior, and not liked. The belief that getting for oneself is greedy and selfish serves as a potent way to remain stuck in self-denial and deprivation.

Self-denial and self-sacrifice are elevated to virtues to hide the secret readiness to feel deprived by the self-indulgence of other people. Inwardly, caterers feel hurt and rejected by the perception that others do not go out of their way to give to them. They feel disappointed and let down by other people's lack of giving and caring towards them. Yet, in their passivity and lack of self-respect, they find it hard to change these circumstances.

There is much confusion over the difference between selfishness and self-care. Selfishness means needing to have things one's own way, demanding to be given to immediately, while insensitive to the feelings and needs of another person. To the selfish person, other people are little more than objects to satisfy his or her own wants and desires. Such people are unable to give because they have not outgrown their infantile egocentric mentality.

In contrast, self-care means honoring and respecting your own wants and needs. It means regarding your feelings and opinions as valid and worthy of consideration. It means not being afraid to pursue your aspirations. Such self-respect is maintained while being considerate and sympathetic to the needs and feelings of others. The self-caring individual is able to compromise and to postpone gratification if necessary. But she still knows it is honorable to want to get for herself. She takes pleasure in receiving as well as giving.

Another way to set yourself up to *not get* is to claim that you do not deserve to get. Inwardly you feel, "Because of my unworthiness, badness, or incompetence,

I do not deserve to get (love, money, acceptance, or acclaim)." If you see yourself as undeserving, you then have an excuse (unconsciously applied, of course) to turn down or refuse to enjoy whatever blessings and opportunities come your way.

Feeling undeserving can ensure that you will fail in life and be forever deprived of meeting your needs and wants. By declining to believe in your self-worth, you hand your fate over to others, and you perpetuate the feeling of being let down, deprived, and dissatisfied. Many people believe that self-denial is a result of low self-worth. Very few people have considered the opposite, that low self-worth can serve as a justification for the indulgence in deprivation and denial.

Who's Been in My Cookie Jar?

Elliot, a wealthy businessman, was in an uproar about the money his second wife had spent. Much of his time and effort went into accounting for their money. All their expenses had to be split down the middle. Everything had to be equal and fair. A prenuptial agreement made sure she would not get any of his "cookies" if they should divorce. Elliot was trying to ward off his inner attachment to being drained, to losing what he had to the spendthrift ways of others.

As a child, he had a younger brother with whom he had to share his toys. He felt his mother favored a younger brother and allowed him to get away with mischief. Elliot, on the other hand, felt punished and deprived. He grew up fearing that other people would take advantage of him and deprive him of what was his. He saw others as "takers" who only wanted to use him. Therefore, psychologically, he had to guard his cookie jar from potential thieves. Feeling that he had lost his mother's love with the birth of his brother, he lived his adult life anticipating the loss of his wealth (mother's

55

love) to others (who represented his brother).

It is typical for people with abundance spend much time worrying about losing it. They anticipate that whatever they have gained will be lost or expropriated by someone. In fact, many people do find themselves the victims of needy relatives, con artists, shady brokers, or "get-rich-quick" schemers who quickly deplete their resources and leave them with an empty cookie jar. Often this happens to people with abundance because they are unwittingly "acting out" their expectations of being victimized.

Most caterers feel uncomfortable receiving and getting.

From childhood, they unconsciously became accustomed to the feeling of being deprived, refused, and denied. They continue to sentence themselves to experiences of emotional deprivation in their adult lives.

One woman realized this and told me: "It's really not that I was denied so much in my childhood. I see now that I learned at a very early age to sacrifice and not give to myself. Taking care of others seemed so easy. I built a structure that turned into a prison, and it became so comfortable that I could not imagine living without it."

Feeling satisfied and fulfilled is an inner experience that is not at all based solely on the reality of what we have. We all know of people who have been content having very little financially. Our ability to feel satisfied depends on the extent to which we are free of attachments to feeling deprived, refused, denied, helpless, criticized, rejected, abandoned, and unloved.

Many individuals, despite receiving everything that others would envy, still are not able to feel satisfied. As long as the individual holds onto an inner attachment to feeling refused or deprived, outer reality will appear as an "empty plate."

All of us live with restrictions, injustices, and

unfairness in our lives. It is how we react to these conditions that determines our emotional wellbeing. Do we see these injustices as taking from us or depriving us? We can use any external circumstance to feel cheated or we can exaggerate feeling deprived out of proportion to the reality of our situation.

Only when we see how focused we are on *not getting* and how we set up our lives to perpetuate feelings of disappointment and emotional deprivation, can we shift our perceptions of life from deprivation and loss to abundance and beauty.

Exercises
Worst-Case Scenarios

Write down your five biggest fears or worries. For each fear or worry, write out your fantasy of the worst thing that could happen. Note the major feelings embedded in each fear.

Trace those feelings back into your life, looking for similar feelings in childhood. For example, if your fear is losing everything you have, recall experiences or perceptions of loss and deprivation in your childhood and describe it. "My parents were always terrified of not having enough money. When I was six, my father lost all his money gambling. It changed our entire lives. I felt helpless, deprived, and humiliated."

Positive Life Scenario

Imagine and write down how you would want things to be if you could manifest your ideal life. Compare it to your life right now. What qualities, values, and feelings are missing from your life that show up in your fantasy life? Reflect on how you are preventing yourself from bringing about your positive life scenario. Blaming others or outside circumstances is not allowed.

Self Denial

- Write down all the ways you can think of that you neglect or deny yourself, for example, with food, spending, relaxation, self-approval, sex. You may include finances, goals, or relationships. Consider instances where you pushed away the chance to get from others.
- What do you feel you missed out on in your life?
- What are your expectations for a happy, fulfilled life? What do you expect from the important people in your life? Are these expectations realistic? If so, how are you sabotaging the attainment of your expectations.
- Do a disappointment inventory. Write out all the disappointments in your life. Include people, places, and things.
- Ask yourself: "Why is it so hard for me to appreciate the good in my life?" Witness the strength of your feelings of deprivation and disappointment and how hard they are to overturn.

Chapter 5
Are We Having Fun Yet?

More irony from the ECS Creed:

- Fantasize the worst possible disaster scenarios and worry about them daily. Revel in the loss and failure of your goals. Reaffirm your belief that your life will be absolutely no fun whatsoever.
- Reject opportunities for pleasure and fun and never get caught enjoying yourself. After all, you would not want to be seen as irresponsible, out of control, or selfish.
- When you catch yourself having a good time, stop immediately. This is the only way to avoid possible shame and rejection.
- Make sure you have a practical reason to justify having a good time, such as, "It's a business trip," or "I'm going to be taking a course which will help my career."
- Anything that is fun or pleasurable is forbidden and must not be allowed. Feeling good is bad.
- Fun is dangerous. You will get hurt if you have too much fun.

What happens to emotional caterers when they go on vacation? Common sense says vacation time is an opportunity to drop all tension and really enjoy yourself. But another side of your personality has other plans that have nothing to do with having fun.

Mary and Bob took a greatly anticipated five-week vacation and drove to California from Florida in their custom van with their eight-year-old son. Their experience raises the question, "What is fun and do we really know how to experience it."

Five miles into the 8,400-mile round-trip, Bob started to worry about money. He was not normally preoccupied with money, and he had brought along plenty of funds for the trip. Nevertheless, he worried about it every day of the five-week vacation. He drove out of his way to find the cheapest gas and constantly complained about gas prices. He worried when his wife shopped, and he declined to buy anything for himself to balance her supposed extravagances. His concerns even applied to food. "Eat up now, stuff yourselves! This way we won't have to stop and eat lunch," he told his family. He worried about every penny that was spent.

During evenings, he drank more alcohol than usual, feeling a need to calm down and relax. He observed in himself a frequent feeling of being short-changed and ripped off. In one motel room where the air-conditioning worked ineffectively, he spent a restless night tormented with the feeling of being a victim of unscrupulous motel owners. On another occasion, he believed the motel owner short-changed him. He spent the next two days composing in his mind an angry letter letting them know what he thought of it. He seethed with the injustice of it all.

Bob experienced the pressure of time, as if he were being forced to "sneak in" a good time, and he became incensed when they were held up in traffic jams. Driving made him irritable, and he spent many anxious hours watching for speed-traps as he travelled the interstate highways. Halfway through the journey he felt a mild panic: he had reached several of his long-awaited destinations but that magic something (fun, joy, pleasure) still eluded him.

Mary, on the other hand, turned the vacation into more work for herself. She worried about every restaurant, rest stop, and motel, even though she had done much advance planning. For her, it was an ordeal to get suitcases in and out of the motel rooms. "Why didn't you get a room on the bottom floor?" she complained. "Now we have to drag all this luggage around." Every time they cooked out, she fell into a serious grumpy mood, became super-efficient and unable to relax. She turned into a drill-sergeant.

Mary planned and scheduled events and sightseeing to make sure they were busy at all times. After all, she did not want to miss out on anything. She exhausted herself and the family trying to take in every sight listed in the travel brochures.

She was creative in producing disaster scenarios. Even before embarking on the trip, she concerned herself with fantasies of doom and destruction. Scenes of flat tires, engine breakdowns, falling off mountain roads, robberies, murder, kidnapping, and getting lost played out in her mind.

How can anyone have fun when they expect it to be taken away at any moment?

Mary also sabotaged her vacation by developing minor but annoying psychosomatic complaints such as constipation, spastic colon, heartburn, headaches, insomnia, and allergic reactions. While climbing on a short hike, she sprained her ankle and was immobile for a few days. On the drive home, she began to worry about the prospect of bad news that awaited them at home.

The problems that Mary and Bob encountered on their vacation were the same issues they encountered in daily life. Bob's big issue was a feeling of being held up or held back in his life. He felt he would never get what he wanted. He associated this feeling with his mother who had not let him walk alone until he was two years old. "Mom always held my hand and wouldn't let me do anything on my own," he said. "The outer world represented danger to my mother, and she was constantly saying how I was going to get hurt, run over, kidnapped, or injured."

Bob felt that his mother had kept him from being spontaneous and from striking out on his own. Even though he had been physically free of his mother for many years, he still perpetuated these feelings of restriction. Bob also connected fun with potential bodily harm and so held himself back as his mother had once held him back.

Mary felt, on an unconscious emotional level, that fun was not allowed. In comparison, work was good. She remembered that, as a child, her favorite activity had been reading novels. Invariably, her dad would find her reading one and say, "Put down that book. Don't you see that we have more important things to do around this house than read books." She had to give up this "frivolity" and go to work. As a result, she had a hard time justifying fun, and so she turned the vacation into a job. Mary also remembered that her father had a miserable time on vacations. He complained incessantly about what was going wrong, and he drank too much. Trying to have fun became a chore.

Mary's and Bob's parents did not deliberately set out to deprive their children of fun. They were brought up with the same attitudes they imparted to their children, and they were unaware of their own inability to enjoy themselves.

An individual on vacation becomes particularly vulnerable because she is supposed to be having fun, a sensation many people know little about. "So why aren't you having more fun," the inner conscience taunts. "You really don't want to enjoy yourself, do you. You'd rather feel that life is struggle and deprivation." Although the individual desperately wishes to be in the present moment enjoying her adventure, she is frequently preoccupied with sabotaging thoughts and fantasies. Why is this so? Why is fun so hard to come by?

We have grown accustomed to feeling denied of fun and pleasure by someone or something. Many of our childhood experiences involved doing household chores, taking care of others, shouldering burdens, and doing schoolwork. Most of us felt that having fun was not encouraged. This belief, learned during childhood, erects barriers to fun and enjoyment in our present lives.

Pam, a 29-year-old secretary, described the origins of her experience with the denial of fun and pleasure. As a child, when she wanted to go out with friends, her father would say, "Don't you know that your mother needs help right now. All you can do is think of yourself and not about how hard we work to put food on the table. You're so selfish."

Once when she had come home ten minutes late from the movies with a friend, her mother barraged her with accusations that she was a "slut" and would come to no good. "That's all you think about, flirting with boys and getting into trouble," her mother yelled. "You never think about us."

After many such experiences, Pam began to associate fun and pleasure with being naughty, bad, shameful, and selfish. When she had a good time, she had to do it covertly, and she lived in fear that someone might discover that she was enjoying herself. She could not allow herself to have fun, and she turned life into a series of chores, along with taking care of others. Even when she did something pleasurable such as taking a vacation, she felt she had to justify it by working overtime to prevent others from judging her as greedy for wanting to have fun.

Her inability to allow herself fun spread into her sex life: Since sex is pleasurable, it must be naughty, forbidden, and not allowed. Pam could not allow herself to enjoy sex or achieve orgasm since pleasure was equated with being bad and selfish.

In fact, she compared enjoying sex and orgasm with the frightening thought of being caught masturbating. She felt she would be hated and condemned.

This connection of fun with the bad and forbidden accounts for some of the attraction of extramarital sex. Since a person is not "allowed" to have sex with another partner and infidelity is considered naughty and bad, people can feel that such dramas are more arousing and sexually stimulating than "permitted" sex with their own spouses. Many people literally "get off" on what is forbidden or what is denied them. For many of us, it seems as if someone is always there to slap our hands whenever we reach out for what we want. The inner voice taunts us with, "You can't have that. That's for others, not you. You have to go without." Thus, we passively accept and endure a lifetime of *not getting* what we want. We deny our right to fun and pleasure and resign ourselves to drudgery and self-imposed service to others.

I have known several clients who experienced anxiety attacks whenever they felt happy or when things were going well. It is a common belief among emotional caterers that it is risky or dangerous to feel happy or get what one desires. Anxiety over happiness or success is the result of an underlying attraction to loss or disappointment. It is the feeling that anything good will always be taken away.

Many of us as children had the experience of liking something that was then taken away. For example, a three-year-old is having a good time splashing in the mud. Mom runs out with disgust, "Oh my, what a mess you've made of yourself. Get out of there this instant. Shame on you!" Or a young girl and her sister are laughing and playing in the back seat of their car on their summer vacation in the mountains. Their dad suddenly yells, "If you two don't stop and keep silent, I'll stop the car and spank the two of you on your behinds." Our past is filled with fun-forbidden episodes we have forgotten.

Admonishments of "don't look, don't kiss, don't laugh, don't run, don't smile, don't touch, don't be foolish" still resonate in our unconscious minds. We associate fun with danger. Such warnings as, "If you go sledding, you'll poke your eye out" and "If you stay out late with your friends, you'll get killed," resound in our ears. As children, we believed that our moms and dads took away our fun because we were having too much pleasure. We "assumed" that they did not want us to like things or enjoy ourselves.

But that is not the primary motive behind parents' restrictions, as I learned when I became a parent. Parents may react out of fear that something will harm their children, or they may be on edge and need peace and quiet. Restrictions exist in all cultures and, for the most part, serve the purpose of socializing the child. Even so, we grow up convinced that "One must not be caught liking certain things." If we like something or enjoy ourselves, we expect it will be taken away and we will experience loss. Or someone will not approve, and we will look bad, out of control, and foolish. So, if we never enjoy anything, then it cannot be taken away, nor can we be looked down upon with disgust for enjoying it.

The Big Bind

"If I experience pleasure or do things that I enjoy, I'll be considered selfish or greedy by others," one client told me. "They won't like me and will resent me for enjoying myself and giving to myself."

With this mentality, fun and pleasure are relinquished. But once a person gives up his pleasure, then he feels cheated out of something he wants. He has an attack of missing out. This swing between being looked down upon as greedy for having too much fun often conflicts with the feeling that we are missing out on fun. Either way we

65

lose.

In order to justify having fun and pleasure, many people feel they have to earn it. This means they feel the need to prove they deserve it or to pay for it somehow. For example, to justify taking a vacation, an individual might feel he must work twice as hard and exhaust himself, so he can claim he really needs the vacation. He feels undeserving of things just because he wants it.

One client, for instance, could only justify going on vacation when he concocted a practical reason. In his mind the vacation had to incorporate business, help a needy relative, or be an opportunity to develop a new skill.

Another way to block fun and pleasure is to harbor great expectations for all the fun one foresees on some future occasion. "Someday in the future my ship will come in," the rationalization goes. "Someday we'll have the time to do what we want and enjoy ourselves." For many individuals that someday never comes. It is tragic to see people work hard all their lives, looking forward to the fruits of their labors, only to have it taken away by bad health or some other unforeseen circumstance. For these people, pleasure and fun have been forever out of reach.

The more an individual dwells on the future, anticipating some joyful bonanza ahead, the more likely he is setting himself up for future disappointment and deprivation, and he misses out on what he could enjoy in the present.

One of my clients dwelled on fantasies of living somewhere else, in some ideal farm-like setting, doing what he had always wanted. He tortured himself with this fantasy, indulging in the feeling of what he could not have. This is a version of the "empty-plate syndrome." Consciously, such a person claims he wants to get, yet inwardly he feels sentenced to a life of drudgery. "Too bad you can't have what you want right now," taunts the inner voice.

Sometimes "dreaming" about future success or prosperity can be a positive aspect of goal-setting. But when the fantasy is unrealistic or is accompanied by feelings of deprival, you are stirring up feelings of dissatisfaction and unhappiness.

Even experiences that are considered "good for us" contain the deprivation element for the person determined to find it. For example, an individual advised to stop abusing alcohol or drugs may feel someone is pulling the milk bottle out of his mouth; a man and woman about to marry can detract from the experience by worrying about all the men and women they have to give up; a person working his way toward a satisfying career may dwell on all the sacrifices he has to make; someone who sees the need to eat better foods to improve his health can begrudge the loss of his junk foods. There are endless ways to wallow in deprival and short-change the prospects of fun and happiness.

Another way to pluck out life's pleasure is to observe and then focus on other people getting all the fun while you have to sit on the sidelines, work, and sacrifice. This is called "peeping" at other people's pleasure in order to accentuate the attachment to feeling deliciously deprived.

One wealthy client was envious that his wife did not have to work. She spent her time playing bridge, having her hair done, golfing, or playing tennis. This man would have continued to work hard at his job and do what he had planned, even if his wife were not in his life. But, in watching her, he was enticed to feel he was not having fun or getting what he wanted.

Most of us associate fun with some kind of action or behavior. We believe it is the external situation or event that creates or causes the feeling of fun. I believe that fun and pleasure are feelings that are generated from within. The feeling is delight or enjoyment in whatever you are

67

doing. Fun or pleasure represent an inner attitude toward the experience you are having.

Blocking this open attitude that life is to be played with and enjoyed is the childhood notion that life should adapt to us and automatically take care of our needs and desires. We try to make others fit our expectations of how they should be and what they should do. We try to impose our needs and wants on others to "make them give us what we want," rather than accept what is given to us and adapt and flow with the circumstances of our lives. Much time and energy is wasted investing in concern about what is not happening in our lives rather than enjoying what is happening.

For many of us in childhood, emphasis was placed on struggle and hard work and on performing to win approval of parents and teachers. Personal accomplishment was emphasized over fun and pleasure. Consequently, we preoccupy ourselves with concern about how others see us. Will they acknowledge me or recognize my accomplishments? Gaining recognition becomes the underlying motivation for our actions rather than an inner belief in the value of our efforts and a sense of personal satisfaction and enjoyment.

It is an art to play at life with an attitude of humor, amusement, and curiosity. The challenge is to disengage the parent within our own minds and to give ourselves permission to enjoy what we have, while pursuing our natural, childlike instinct for spontaneity and wonder.

Exercise

Write down or think about what fun or pleasure means to you? What did it mean as a child? How was fun or pleasure blocked in your childhood. What were your parents' attitudes toward fun and pleasure?

What is stopping you now from having more enjoyment and fun in your life?

Chapter 6
To Control or be Controlled: That's the Issue

ECS Creed:
- Allow others to dominate you, push you around, and make decisions for you. Remember that your life is at the disposal of others. Take comfort in the thought that your compliance "makes them feel great."
- Endure unpleasant situations rather than take action. Try to see how much mistreatment or neglect you can take without getting upset.
- Use the excuses, "He or she won't let me be myself" or "They'll get mad" in order to avoid being yourself or doing what you want.
- Do not take any initiative in your life; wait until a break comes along. Blame your failures on bad luck, money problems, or too many responsibilities.
- Before embarking on an endeavor, imagine the worst that can happen and allow that to stop you.
- Make sure you do not know what you want, then accuse others of not giving it to you.

"I have no control over my life," exclaimed a caterer. "I'm so overwhelmed with pressures and obligations, I'll never get to do what I want." As that comment suggests, emotional caterers are accustomed to feeling dominated and controlled, despite their apparent need to control others.

Control issues begin to surface when a child is eighteen months to three years old. As many parents are aware, children at that age resist toilet training or attempts to turn them into civilized beings. The child takes personal offense when his parents tell him what to do and how to do it. Children may scream and protest against feeling controlled and dominated. Even the most gentle parents feel frustrated at their attempts to train their toddlers.

It seemed to us that childhood consisted of passive experiences of giving up what we wanted and going along with someone else's will. Our childhood was filled with have to's: *have to go to* bed, *have to* eat my vegetables, *have to* get dressed, *have to* clean up my room, and *have to* be good. We felt forced or coerced to submit to our parents and to life. As adults, we experience similar feelings of having to submit to life, to comply with the needs of others, and to perform the chores of daily life.

Many of us felt as children that we had little influence on the feelings and behaviors of our parents and passively had to endure threatening or neglectful situations. We were rewarded for controlling our emotions and impulses. We were loved if we obeyed without protest. Compliance meant love and acceptance. It was our actions and behaviors that were deemed important and not our feelings. Consequently, we learned to close down our feelings and experience ourselves through activity.

We tend to define ourselves by what we *do* rather than how we *feel*. Feelings were experienced as alien, unwanted intrusions that brought on rejection and disapproval.

As adults, caterers fear being out of control. Being out of control means losing our ability to repress or hide our strong emotional feelings or appearing to be less than perfect in the eyes of others. Being out of control feels like giving in or being weak and vulnerable. It brings up buried feelings of worthlessness and powerlessness.

Consequently, caterers develop a need to control our environment and everyone in it. This need to control

71

reflects the need to keep our world safe by minimizing or avoiding unacceptable thoughts, feelings, and behaviors in ourselves as well as in others. This is a form of repression, accomplished by managing, lecturing, and supervising other people's behaviors and reactions.

This need to be in charge and manage other people's lives hides the unconscious attachment to feeling forced to submit to the will of others. As long as we control every aspect of our own lives, along with the lives of others, we create an illusion of independence. But if we are not in charge, then we tend to feel dominated and controlled. There is little gray area or balance between these two extremes.

Since the attachment to being dominated and controlled is not appealing in yourself, you cover it up in different ways. You can become defiant. Whatever your parents wanted you to be, you decide to become the opposite. Sam, at 44, found himself without a relationship, children, or a stable career. He bemoaned the lack of success in his life. His father was a wealthy, successful businessman who wanted him to be a money-making "professional," with an attractive wife and children. He wanted Sam to imitate his lifestyle.

From the beginning, Sam rebelled and defied his father's authority. Though he was highly intelligent, he got poor grades, which made his father furious. Sam sabotaged his college career and ended up in dead-end business ventures. He claimed he could not work in a normal job because he couldn't bear submitting to someone else's will.

Sam never married. He chose to become involved with married women or party girls. He did not want to end up like his parents, so defiance became the motivating force in his life. Sam felt he had to live outside his parents' value system to "be himself." Unfortunately, it cost him dearly; he became lonely and financially destitute.

Success and happiness for Sam meant submission to his father's will.

Sandy, a secretary, struggled with weight problems for years. She couldn't figure out why her dieting attempts always failed. As a child, her mother controlled Sandy's food and clothes. Her mother had fussed excessively over Sandy's appearance.

Sandy unconsciously frustrated her mother's efforts by retaining the weight. As an adult, when it would have been in her best interest to lose the weight, she sabotaged herself, not wanting to submit or give in to her mother's will. Being overweight was the only way Sandy knew to preserve her identity.

As these examples show, you can defeat yourself in order to "prove" your dislike for being controlled. Some people experience themselves as alive and strong only when they are in opposition to others. Even though defiance gives them a feeling of independence, they remain controlled by an inner agenda that leaves them frustrated and powerless.

Another way to defend against feeling controlled is to avoid situations that lead to the possibility of feeling controlled. Avoidance rather than defiance now becomes a lifestyle. Such individuals hop from one situation to another, one relationship to another, to avoid the emotional challenges of commitments. They regard isolation and self-sufficiency as the criteria of independence. "I don't need anyone," they claim. "I take care of myself. I don't need to rely or be dependent on anyone. I can do everything myself."

This role is called "counter-dependency," a behavior that allows an individual to feel he is in the driver's seat, the one whom others depend on. A counter-dependent has great fear of depending on others and regards feelings or need as signs of weakness and worthlessness. By assuming a superior, know- it-all position, he

73

discourages others from giving to him or helping him. Receiving or seeking help are associated with being inadequate and feeling controlled. In his past, he felt as if approval from his parents was gained only when he was submissive or obliging. Now he associates being dependent on others with humiliation and submission.

You also can attempt to disown your passivity and attachment to being controlled by adopting a controlling personality. Here are some characteristics that describe this personality:

* You are critical and focus on other people's faults or weaknesses.

* You give unsolicited advice or help and feel frustrated or unappreciated when people do not follow your advice.

* You cannot take criticism and you react defensively when someone points out your weaknesses.

* You like to decide what others should do, jump right in, and make decisions for them. You are convinced your way is the right way.

* You are not really interested in the perspectives or feelings of others. You often don't hear their point of view or let them express their feelings. Sometimes you put down their feelings or ideas and inwardly feel their feelings are misguided.

* You get upset when others refuse you or say no to your requests. You get upset when others fail to change and become the way you want them to be.

* You are hesitant to reveal and express your own personal feelings. You are convinced you are "all-together" and do not need help.

* You lecture, nag, and hammer away at others until they give in and comply.

* You have a need to convince others of the "correctness" of your position. You communicate solely to make a point or win an argument.

* You often use other authorities to justify your position. "So and so (books, Bible, articles) says you are wrong." The assumption here is that higher authorities agree with *your* position.

* You are likely to shout, hurl insults, shame, and make the other person feel bad in order to get him to comply with your demands.

* When others disagree, you feel they are against you and you feel betrayed. You are apt to get angry or withdraw should others go against your wishes.

* You have a need for perfect order (the house, the kids, your plans for the day), and you become upset when this order is disrupted.

The need to control others serves several objectives: It 1) gets others to satisfy your emotional needs for attention and recognition, 2) allays your own fears and insecurities, 3) covers up the terror of depending on others who will let you down, and 4) masks feelings of being vulnerable, powerless, and at the mercy of situations you cannot control.

The need to control others also represents a need to control yourself, that is, your own emotions, thoughts, and behaviors. In controlling others, you are under the illusion of being in control of yourself. "If I am not controlling others," a client remarked, "I would feel out of control. I would feel weak and ineffectual." With a weak sense of self, controlling others provides an identity, a purpose for living.

On a conscious level, you strive for freedom and independence, but the child part of your psyche remains trapped in the belief that life means giving up what you want in order to accommodate the agendas of others. Hence, you spend your life dreaming of a time when you can be free to be yourself (as you did when you were a child), while devising excuses for not acting out your deepest aspirations.

An emotionally independent person does not have to "prove" that she is in control. She simply does what she wants, without making a big protest, or she submits graciously when appropriate, because it is in her best interest to do so. Her power resides in her integrity and in her deep sense of self-worth. Consequently, whether to control or be controlled is not an issue.

She understands that limitation is part of life and that there is no way to escape from being controlled by outside circumstances. Nor can she make life conform to her needs and expectations or resolve her fears. She realizes that freedom is an inner feeling she gives herself. She accepts that life and relationships entail give and take, compromise and surrender. She surrenders not out of weakness or fear, but out of grace and wisdom.

Signs of Passivity

Caterers express both controlling behavior and passive, dependent behavior. Usually they alternate between the two extremes. They may be controlling at work and passive with their spouses or controlling at home and passive at work. They can be passive at some stage in their lives and controlling at other periods. They tend to be passive when it would be in their best interest to assert themselves, and controlling when it is not appropriate or productive.

The following are passive behaviors that indicate an underlying attachment to being controlled and dominated. The attachment to being controlled was established in childhood. Notice that these behaviors are replays of the parent-child relationship. In other words, you transfer your passivity, your dependency and your fears from your parents onto your present-day relationships.

An inability to say no or stand up for yourself. Many caterers find it impossible to say *no* to others. They are unable to draw boundaries or assert their wants and needs. They go along with the opinions of others even when they disagree. They become so accustomed to accommodating others that they are not even aware of their own passivity.

For thirty years, Judy allowed her husband to pick out her clothes, decide when she could visit her friends, choose food on menus, and so on. Whatever she wanted, she felt the need to seek his permission. Disagreement or refusal were unknown responses for her. Occasionally, she sneaked out to shop, all the while feeling guilty, as if some invisible force was urging her to rush home.

"It was easy to let him take responsibility for everything," Judy explained. "I didn't have to make any decisions. It's hard for me now to take responsibility for myself. I want others to tell me what to do. I need someone in my life to control me." Her husband required her to be with him at all times, just as her mother had when she was a child. Judy was reliving her passive relationship with her dominating mother, perpetuating feelings of being owned and controlled. Her mother had never tolerated a defiant reaction. For years, until friends convinced her something was wrong, Judy believed her husband's control was normal. In time, Judy began to speak up and assert herself.

In another case, Holly finally got up the nerve to say *no* to her mother's demands. "Saying no to her was the most difficult thing I've ever done," she remarked. "I felt as if I were abandoning her and that I was responsible for keeping her alive. I expected her to die if I didn't take care of her."

Holly felt she had no choice in childhood but to take care of her mother. Her mother had begged her to stay home rather than go out with her friends. In Holly's mind, she heard her mother pleading, "Please, don't leave me. I need you. I don't
know what I'd do without you."

Holly was locked in a symbiotic embrace with her mother. If she took care of mother, then Holly would be loved and approved of. But if she exercised her independent wishes and desires, she would be considered bad and rejected. Her mother did abandon her emotionally in childhood, not speaking to her for days after Holly had been out with friends. Holly felt she had no choice but to endure her mother's neediness and put her own needs last. She concluded that she was not meant to be happy. Being herself meant that she had no value to anyone.

As an adult, Holly acted out the role of rescuer. She entangled herself in the lives of others. She only felt validated when someone needed her. When they appeared not to need her, she believed they would leave her. Yet she felt suffocated and dominated by their needs and wanted out of these relationships to preserve her own integrity.

Feelings of love were elusive. If she were to love someone, she feared he would abandon her. To avoid the hurt of rejection and abandonment, Holly left her partners before they left her.

Attempts at emotional independence brought out guilt for "abandoning" her mother. She carried the responsibility for her mother's wellbeing and happiness over into her adult life, thereby quelling independent autonomous feelings or expressions. In "buying into" her mother's claim that she was responsible for her mother's happiness, Holly continued her unconscious program of being oppressed and dominated by the needs of others.

Her guilt covered up the real problem—her attachment to being held captive in her mother's powerful embrace. Guilt for "abandoning" her mother also masked her lingering attachment to the feeling of having been abandoned by her mother in childhood. Holly was struggling with two major attachments, the attachment to feeling engulfed, suffocated, and dominated by the needs of others and the attachment to being abandoned and unloved.

Here is another example of passivity that results in self-neglect. Lou Ann blamed her husband for not allowing her to go back to school to advance her career. She had been holding onto this grudge for years but took no action to manifest her aspirations.

When she finally confronted her husband with his apparent denial of her wishes, he was taken aback. He said he had never refused her opportunities to better herself. In fact, he insisted, she had never even raised the issue with him. If she had, he said, he would have had no objection to her wish to go back to school. Lou Ann said she never asked because she knew he would refuse. Since he had refused her and controlled her in other ways, she expected him to do so again in this situation.

Lou Ann used her husband as a cover for her own passive tendencies. Her husband's alleged dominance also covered up her fears of failure and perpetuated feelings of being controlled and restricted. As Lou Ann expressed it, "I gave up my life for someone else to control. I wanted to believe that he denied me the expression of myself and forbade me to speak up. I see now that *I chose to believe* that I had no choice but to suppress myself."

She had felt "bound up" and "pinned down" by the demands of others, as she had in childhood with her mother. Her mother had convinced her it was foolish for a woman to go to college. Lou Ann unconsciously transferred this attitude onto her husband, perpetuating feelings of being deprived and controlled.

Caterers do not assert themselves nor share the truth of how they feel because they allow themselves to be controlled and tyrannized by another person's emotional responses. Going along with the agenda of others acts as an insurance policy against being rejected, unloved, or seen as wrong. Caterers rationalize their passivity by claiming, "I'm only trying to keep the peace" or, "I don't want to hurt anyone's feelings." Unfortunately, the compulsive quest for the favor of others results in the surrender of one's autonomy.

Not knowing what you want. Another way to invite domination is to be in the dark about what you want or need. This opens the door for others to come in and influence your thoughts, emotions, and behaviors. Not knowing what you want also serves as a way to avoid the possibility of failure. Failure can happen when you try to attain something. If you do not know what you want or have aspirations, you can feel at least you have not failed. Unfortunately, you cannot succeed either.

Fear of making the wrong decision. This fear expresses another way to avoid taking charge of your life. To avoid the responsibility of making your own decisions, you may run around frantically seeking advice from friends, doctors, teachers, or psychics. If you get others to tell you what to do (passivity), then you can blame them when their advice does not work. This absolves you from accountability for your actions.

Another way to remain passive is to flood yourself with too many choices, all equally viable, and then be unable to make up your mind. Consequently, you go nowhere.

Do nothing or fail. A common passive behavior is to do nothing. You can maintain your level of passivity by not initiating projects on your own, by enduring situations, ignoring problems, not following through, isolating yourself, getting sick, losing yourself in television or a book, or numbing the issues with alcohol, drugs, or food.

Doing nothing, or failing to take action to realize your goals, invites other people or fate to take control. This is exactly what the passive person unconsciously seeks—to be dominated, controlled, and told what to do.

Automatic compliance to the demands of others. Terry was a successful owner of his own business. At work, he had no problem asserting his wants and directing others. Yet at home he had serious difficulty standing up to his wife. Terry saw her as nagging, demanding, bossy, and needy. Whatever she asked of him, he felt he had no choice but to comply. Terry used the excuse, "She'll erupt in a rage," to justify his passive compliance and feelings of being oppressed. He stewed inside with anger and had frequent fantasies of leaving her.

But that would not solve his passive tendency to submit to his wife or someone else with whom he crossed paths. If he did not resolve this problem, he was more than likely to repeat this pattern in his next relationship.

Terry was reliving, through his wife, his relationship with his father. His father had been strict, controlling, and demanding of swift obedience, while Terry had meekly complied. This pattern of compliance and accommodation followed Terry in his personal relationships. Until he started therapy, he had been unaware of his passivity. He simply believed compliance was normal.

As Terry gained "insight" into his compliance, he began to speak up and assert his own wishes and needs to his wife. Their relationship improved as his wife softened and became less demanding, while his feelings of aggravation and anger diminished.

If you suspect you are like Terry, ask yourself, "Why do I feel I must comply with other people's terms? Why do I find it so easy to sacrifice my own wishes and desires to please them? Who does this person remind me of from my past? In what other areas of my life do I respond in a compliant, accommodating fashion? Remember, no one can control you or make you do anything unless you allow them to have that power over you.

Giving power to authority figures. Caterers display a fear of authority figures. Lorrie, for one, felt she was living in a police state. She perceived her boss as a reincarnated Nazi who scrutinized her work, intent on finding mistakes. Periodically, he called her into his office to criticize her efforts and warn her about the consequences of not doing better. This was how she had felt as a child with her father. She felt she had no emotional "immune system."

For many, job situations provide a replay of the powerlessness experienced in childhood. This is because the boss, with all his power, triggers unconscious memories of parents who also had power and control. Like a child who felt she had no choice but to submit, an adult continues feeling powerless and at the mercy of others who are felt to have all the power.

Many of us fear asserting our beliefs or exercising our personal power because we associate power with hurting others. We do not have a positive perception of power. Either we feel the victim of the Gestapo or, if we use our power, we feel like (and maybe act like) the Gestapo. Being powerful is equated with being mean, insensitive, and indifferent about others. This is how we perceived our powerful parents.

As long as you are dependent on "authorities" for answers about your own life, you will not be able to become your own authority. Consequently, you perpetually set yourself up to be controlled and dominated by others.

Caterers fear to trust in themselves. They feel helpless without something concrete to rely on. To trust oneself brings up fears of making mistakes and being seen by others as inadequate and foolish. For many, having someone control and direct their lives gives them the feeling of being supported. They feel reassured that they will not be abandoned or neglected.

The caterer doth protest too much. Passive individuals have a tendency to store up grievances and erupt in explosive outbursts. Such outbursts are protests against unconscious attachments to feeling controlled or victimized. They are defensive reactions rather than genuine attempts at conflict resolution. This is the defense: "How can anyone suggest that I want to be passively dominated and pushed around by others? Can't you see how much I hate it? I'm not going to let anyone shove me around anymore."

Any such defense or protest indicates you really are attached to the feeling of being pushed around by the expectations and demands of others. You would not spend so much energy proclaiming your autonomy if you had not already relinquished it. Autonomous or independent people do not go around protesting against being controlled because they do not feel they are being controlled, even in situations where others might be trying to control them.

Usually aggressive protests are out of proportion to the alleged transgression. For example, a wife looks forward to her husband coming home for dinner. He is twenty minutes late. When he comes in, the wife innocently says, "Hi honey, did you have to work overtime tonight?" He replies in a rage, "Why do you always have to question me like this when I come home? You're always accusing me of doing something wrong. I can't take this anymore. You're just like your mother." He storms into his study, slams the door, and shuts her out for the rest of the evening.

This man's defensive reaction reveals his propensity to feel accused and criticized. Even if his wife were a shrew, his reaction is still counter-productive and defensive, rather than aimed at clarifying his position and his feelings. He is unconsciously attached to the notion of being held captive and dominated by a commanding shrew who holds him accountable. Otherwise, he would respond to his wife's question without such a defensive display.

Defensive, angry outbursts are indications of underlying guilt, fear, and insecurity. Anger is usually a reaction to the existence of an underlying feeling such as hurt, rejection, betrayal, neglect, criticism, or control. Once you understand your addiction to these underlying emotions and where they come from in your past, you automatically learn not to react so personally. Anger diminishes on its own once you "see" more objectively and feel more secure in yourself.

Passive ineffective communication. Communicating in a passive manner also indicates an underlying attachment to feeling dominated, intimidated, and controlled. Most caterers have a hard time asking for help, or asking questions to clarify another's intent. They do not pursue information they need to know, fearing that they will look stupid. They fear and avoid confrontations, discussions, or arguments because they might lose or look bad. They are uncomfortable sharing vulnerable feelings, fearing these will be used against them or that they will be perceived as weak. They share a belief that speaking one's feelings hurts others or invites disaster. Consequently, these beliefs set them up to be dominated and controlled.

An Unresponsive Man

Jenny, a 49-year-old housewife, complained that her husband never shared his feelings or let her know where he stood on important issues. He talked only about superficial, daily matters. The more she tried to get him to open up and discuss personal matters, the more he clammed up.

In frustration, she exclaimed to me, "I feel like I have to pull things out of him. He just won't respond. Every time I try to talk with him about feelings he either leaves the room, stares at the TV, or changes the subject. He tries to avoid any kind of encounter with how he really feels. I feel he's not really there for me. He never asks me questions about what I'm experiencing. I feel he isn't interested in me. How else can I interpret this behavior but to believe that he doesn't care at all about me? He simply doesn't see me. I take his refusal to talk as an indication he really doesn't want to give to me. If only he'd share with me and tell me what he feels, I'd respect him a lot more."

Her husband, Jack, a 52-year-old businessman, told me in an individual session, "If I said what I really felt, she'd go into a rage. She'd never accept my feelings or opinions on things. It would only make things worse. My only choice is to ride the storm and hope it blows away fast, or pretend it's really not
happening. When we talk, it feels like she's arguing or complaining.

"How do arguments or complaints make you feel?" I asked.

"It makes me withdraw even more from her and put up a wall," he responded. "Now the wall's so thick, I don't know if it could ever come down. Even when things are okay, I feel like I have to be careful and tip-toe around her. Anything can set her off. I live with this constant fear that she'll erupt and attack me with some kind of ridiculous complaint. I never know what kind of mood she'll be in. I also feel that arguments will cause her to hate me and perhaps even leave me."

"It sounds like you believe Jenny isn't really interested in your feelings," I remarked.

"That's true. She's really not interested in what I feel. Her discussions are just an excuse to beat on me. She's always looking for an excuse to put me down. I'm never good enough, or adequate enough to satisfy her. Nobody could satisfy her. I feel rejected by her. Why should I give her what she wants when she won't accept me as I am? I feel like I'm always being evaluated and judged. Besides, I can't stand it that she expects me to produce, perform, or give to her on demand. I want it to be my choice. If I give into her, I feel like I'm submitting, that she wins."

"Is this situation with your wife similar to your childhood in any way?"

"It's quite the same," he said thoughtfully. "It was downright sinful to speak back to my parents. I had to take whatever they dished out. I was never allowed to have feelings, much less express them. I endured many judgmental lectures and verbal harangues dealing with my supposed inadequacies and misbehaviors, some of which I'm sure I provoked. But it was the same terror and fear I experience today. I believed that there was no way they would accept my point of view or understand me. I believed my parents would hate me and disown me forever if they knew the truth of how I really felt. My feelings were always wrong. My only recourse was to stuff it, endure it, and imagine it not happening. I don't see that I had any other options."

Jack was no longer a child and his wife was not his mother. On an emotional level, however, he repeated the passive child role that he played with his parents. He recreated feelings of being chastised and criticized that he had experienced as a child, and he expected his wife to respond to him in the same critical manner that his parents did. He indulged in feelings of being intimidated by someone else's critical judgments and outbursts. Unconsciously, he had made a choice to be dominated and tyrannized by his wife's anger and disapproval.

Though it was acceptable to speak up and express his feelings, Jack still responded as though he were being held back and bound up by his parents. He anticipated being unloved and abandoned for revealing his true feelings. Ironically, the more he failed to respond to Jenny, the more he risked having her leave him. As long as he remained unresponsive, he would continue to feel oppressed and intimidated.

"If only she wouldn't harp at me, I would respond and share my feelings," Jack protested. He blamed her for his lack of response, but in secret he used her negative reactions as justifications to "withhold," thereby avoiding responsibility for his passive behavior and his attachment to abandonment. Jack's lack of ability to respond had nothing to do with Jenny.

He was unconsciously withholding to retaliate against his parents (and now Jenny) for allegedly not accepting him and being present to his needs. How could he give her what he never received from his family? Jack was also unconsciously complying with the family law, "Shut up and never express your true feelings."

Communication had been superficial in Jack's family of origin. He perceived that his parents had no real interest in him other than in making him conform to their will. He retaliated by disobeying them. This tit-for-tat game, later played out with Jenny, covered up something deeper in Jack—his indulgence in being emotionally neglected and forced to perform according to the will of others.

Meanwhile, Jenny interpreted her husband's emotional withholding as defiance and rejection. She chose to believe he deliberately refused her because he wanted to hurt her. She contended her emotional harangues were necessary to get him to open up and "confess." But the more she tried to "extract" his feelings, the more he refused to comply. Actually, she reinforced the pattern of withdrawal in her husband. Her manner of communication represented an intrusive manipulation to allay her own feelings of insecurity, rather than a genuine expression of

87

caring.

Jenny was trying to squeeze juice out of a dried-up orange, a replay of her experience with both parents. This fruitless endeavor promoted her ongoing indulgence in feelings of being deprived and withheld from. Replaying their childhood hurts off each other only served to keep them both stuck in recycled patterns of pain.

Jack was not withholding to torture Jenny. His communication problem was not motivated by an intention to reject her. He was stuck in a passive pattern of relating, which he did not understand. He was not even aware that he was not really seeing her or being present to her. Unconsciously, he was seeing her as a cold and demanding parent. He automatically withheld emotionally as he had with his parents. He simply did not have a program for direct, honest, and defensive-free communication with others.

Here are several other patterns of communication that prevent honest and clear expressions of feelings. These patterns of communication will intensify your feelings of being controlled by others.

- Whining and complaining turn people off and ensure they won't listen to you.
- Speaking meekly, without conviction, and never initiating discussions, ensures that others will not take you seriously.
- Giving evasive answers such as, "Not necessarily" or, "I don't know how I feel" makes others want to tell you how to live your life.
- Never bringing problems or issues to completion or resolution, as well as shoving problems under the carpet or dismissing them as "no big deal," leaves you feeling helpless and at the mercy of circumstances.
- Communicating in a rambling fashion, changing the subject, going off on another tangent, refusing to

get to the point, or taking things out of context rarely result in clarification of what you want.

- You also let others take over and control you when you don't ask relevant questions, or when you jump to negative assumptions and conclusions without verification.
- You will not achieve understanding or solve your personal issues when you talk behind a person's back. You want to learn to talk directly to the person you are having a problem with.
- Beware of borrowing other people's opinions or feelings, even when you do not accept those opinions and feelings. Ask yourself, why is it so hard to express my own opinions?
- Sometimes you may give up on communication, feeling it does no good, and that others do not listen anyhow. Or you may always be apologizing, even when others hurt your feelings.
- Always defending and explaining yourself usually leaves others feeling they are right and you are wrong.

Most people talk at each other rather than listen to each other. They try to make a point or win an argument and fail to understand the other's point of view. They do not see the other person as he or she is because they focus emotionally and mentally on themselves and their inner insecurities.

No genuine communication occurs with domination and intimidation. Nor can you see the other person clearly if you are needing something from him. In most communication, people are formulating their arguments or disagreements rather than being present and listening to the other person. They are too interested in getting the other person to see it their way or do what they want. Or they may be communicating to make themselves feel superior. When people are always defending their own positions, true feelings are not communicated.

Most communication is used as a means to control others or win a point. Many people can't keep their mouths shut and listen because they are so eager to influence or impress the other person. Even passive communication or withholding of words can be used to manipulate others to get what you want. For example, a person goes along with others to allay his fears of not being liked; he submits to win favor.

True listening requires an interest in the other person's point of view. This way we learn something about each other rather than personalizing what is said. We explore problems together, like a team. This kind of communication has no personal agenda. Foremost is genuine curiosity about the other person's perceptions or feelings. You are open to what he says. You ask questions such as, "How do you see this issue? How are you feeling about this situation? How do you feel about me? Do you have any ideas on how we can resolve this problem?"

A good communicator lets the other person ventilate feelings, and often does not offer advice unless the other person asks for it.

In summary, caterers anxiously try to control their environment to forestall being victims of some unforeseen circumstances. On an inner emotional level, they are like strangers in a strange land. They feel lost without the guidance of others. They feel they cannot be themselves, and they feel the need for some outside influence directing their lives.

To counter his attachment to being powerless and controlled by others, the caterer creates the illusion that he causes what happens to him and to others in his life. He tries to maintain a feeling of being in control by managing and fixing everybody and everything in his life. If he fails to manage others smoothly, he accuses himself of negligence, of letting others down. He indulges in endless refrains of, "If only I'd done better" or "Why didn't I think of that." These refrains intensify feelings of being powerless and at the mercy of forces that he cannot control.

An emotionally independent person is in control of his life. He or she does not feel the need to control other people or life's events. Control is simply not an issue. He accepts that there will be situations or people he cannot control. He does not react personally to controlling situations, but manages them the best way he can.

Exercise

Passivity and Control

For one to three days, go through the day thinking about everything you do and ask yourself, "Is this what I want to do right now?" For every action you take, ask yourself, "Is this my decision, my choice? What do I want to do next?" Be aware of how much of your daily actions consist of passive compliance or unconscious choices.

Experiment with going through your day saying, "I *have to*... with every action or chore, compared with going through your day saying, "I *choose to*..." with every action or chore.

- Write a history of how you let other people or situations influence or dominate you.
- Who has made the major decisions in your life?
- Name the outside authorities you consult for answers or validation.
- List missed opportunities or situations where you sabotaged success.
- Write down the major ways you feel controlled and powerless. How do you react to these situations?
- Note down as many of your controlling behaviors as you can think of. Who do you try to control and why?

- Write about feelings of being powerless and controlled as a child. What parent had the most power over you? How did your parents control you? How did you react to being controlled as a child?
- Imagine going through one day without trying to control your surroundings or other people. Now actually do it. See if you can experience one day letting go of your need to control. Write down every time you get the urge to control someone or something. What feelings come up for you? Where do they come from in your past?

Here is another exercise that helps readers learn to listen and be present to what others are communicating.

- Listen to another person from the perspective of a detached witness for five, ten, fifteen minutes. Do not talk about yourself. Merely listen to what the other person is saying and how he is saying it.
- Notice what subjects he talks about. Notice any revealing emotions he expresses. At the same time, become aware of how you feel while listening. How do you react to what you see and hear?
- How hard is it for you to be a detached observer and simply allow certain incidents or situations to run their course?

Chapter 7
ECS to The Rescue: "I'm Only Trying to Help"

ECS Creed:
- Ask yourself daily, how many people did you "save" today or steer onto the "right path?" Others do not know what is best for them. Only you have the right answers.
- Always give advice or suggestions, especially when they are not solicited.
- Give to others even when it means sacrifice to yourself. Take pride in your self-denial.
- Do for others what they really can do for themselves. Do whatever you can to ensure they love you.
- Refuse to take account of your own emotional issues by making the other person out to be the "sick" one. Make it a project to straighten him out and get him to face up to his weakness.

One way to avoid being controlled and dominated by others is to control and dominate them. However, the blatant control of others is not acceptable behavior. Consequently, a more subtle form of controlling is needed, one that disguises the control.

The answer is to become a rescuer and take on the burden for the progress, development, and happiness of others. Rescuing people at your own personal expense results in a life-long association with an assortment of "alley cats." Emotional caterers leave the door wide open for strays to enter and thereby ensure further opportunities for their own self-denial.

One caterer put it this way: "I saw others and society

in the same way that I saw my alcoholic father. I was going to reform them, set them straight, and inject them with the rationality that I saw so lacking in my father. By getting Dad to change, then maybe I wouldn't feel so helpless and ignored."

Orchestrating the Experiences of Others

One sign of a rescuer mentality is an undue concern for other people's problems and an urgency to do something about them. This attitude can take the form of unsolicited advice, recommended books, and the urge to point others in the "right" direction.

Assuming the authority of an ordained minister, the rescuer claims to know what is best. "If only they would take my advice, their whole lives would turn around," the rescuer contends. "I know what they need to do."

She reads a few self-help books and becomes an "expert" in the art of "being human." Now when people do not respond to her recommendations or suggestions, she becomes upset. Or she discounts the "resistant" individual with a statement such as, "She's in incredible denial." One sure sign of a rescuing mentality is the reaction, "I really don't think this applies to me (books or articles describing catering behavior), but I sure can see how it applies to a lot of people I know."

This preoccupation with the lives of others takes the focus off your own emotional issues. Focusing on others also provides an artificial boost of self-esteem, as well as the illusion that you are in control.

Sometimes a rescuer has recurrent fantasies of possessing special powers or knowledge that will save others and the world from misery. He will entice others into his brand of therapy or spiritual endeavors. As a "savior" he wants to take away the pain of others, not out of compassion but to redeem his own flagging sense of self-worth. Those who refuse his form of salvation are regarded as lost souls.

Adopting the superior position of knowing what is wrong with others and having the right answers, covers up the secret attachment to feeling unimportant and ignored. Rescuers are often looking for cosmic validation of their worth. The need to impress one's views or ideology on others in the name of "helping" is a disguised form of domination and control that is motivated by an inner conviction of unworthiness.

Here is how one caterer expressed it: "If I am not right, then I feel worthless. I only exist to serve the needs of others. If I don't serve or help them, then I've no validity. If I don't help to change them, I take it to mean there's something wrong with me."

A rescuer also has another secret agenda—getting others to acknowledge their hidden weaknesses and face up to their flaws. This desire to make others accountable is self-serving and reflects an unconscious attachment on the part of the rescuer to being a victim of the irresponsibility and weakness of others. This is an old feeling that goes back to his childhood experience with his parents.

As I have said, a caterer cannot accept others the way they are for his own personal reasons. Foremost is his attempt to avoid experiencing the uncomfortable feelings people trigger in him.

Let us use an example. As a child, you come home from school and find your mom severely depressed. You react by feeling threatened, scared, abandoned, helpless, or ignored. Such feelings are intense and uncomfortable. You try to control the situation by 1) assuming you are responsible for your mother's bad mood and 2) trying to fix your mother and make her feel good. Once she feels good, you do not have to feel threatened and helpless.

You believe that other people cause you to react or feel the way you do. This puts you at the mercy of their moods and behaviors. You are dependent on the happiness of others in order to be happy yourself. Since you believe the other person is responsible for the feelings you are having, you want the other person to change. Changing him or her, so you believe, eliminates the unpleasant feelings and reactions you are experiencing.

It is far more productive to understand the origins of your reactions to the behaviors of others. Ask yourself, "Why do I want this person to change? Why do I want them to lose weight, or get help, or become happy? Why is it so important to me that they learn to take care of themselves the way I want them to? What will I get if they change? What do I feel if they do not change?" Explore your feelings about the other person and your motivations for wanting him to be different.

If you are in the helping professions, ask yourself, "What is your motive for wanting to help others? What will helping others give you? Why is it so important that others agree or go along with your approach to growth?

A Rescuer in Action

Sally, a 36-year-old nurse, was married to Bob, an easy-going fellow with less education. Bob allowed Sally to do what she wanted and seldom made demands. However, Sally experienced herself as a victim of Bob's weaknesses. She complained of his drinking, his nonchalance, his inability to be intimate, and his lack of ambition.

Sally devised a program to make Bob a stronger person. She supplied him with books, articles, and suggestions, and she badgered him to attend personal growth groups as well as therapy. Bob took offense, interpreting her pressure as an indication he was not good enough. He felt nagged at and controlled. "I can't do anything right," he exclaimed.

Sally wanted Bob to change because she believed his

weakness caused her to feel deprived and depressed. She felt he was not living up to his potential or progressing fast enough in his career. Meanwhile, it felt that she had to shoulder the responsibility of the household. It seemed to her that Bob had the luxury to do whatever he wanted, while she had no choice but to work hard and give up her creative pursuits.

In some ways, Bob reminded Sally of her father, who was dominating and had often become critical and judgmental of others. Her father failed to live up to his potential and had sabotaged his career by drinking too much. Sally had felt discounted, powerless, and humiliated by his emotional rages and his criticism of her. He had frequently accused her of laziness, especially when he saw her doing something enjoyable.

Sally unconsciously had chosen easy-going Bob to avoid being controlled by a dominating, insensitive person like her father. In her marriage, she became like her father and subjected Bob to the same treatment that she had received from her father. She tried to change Bob by being just as critical and judgmental to him as her father had been to her. She was unaware that her efforts made the situation worse. Her need to transform Bob masked her entanglement in the familiar feelings of being powerless, controlled, and abandoned that she had experienced with her father.

The more pressure Sally put on Bob to change, the more he resisted. The more he resisted, the more she felt unappreciated and a victim of his nonchalance. In Sally's eyes, he refused to give her the emotional support that she gave him.

Although she was in a dominant position in her marriage, she felt as controlled and oppressed by Bob's passivity as she had felt controlled by her dominating father. With both, she felt offended by their indifference and abandoned by their lack of responsiveness to her

97

needs.

"But what do I do about Bob," she asked me, "just let him do what he wants?"

"You will not find relief from your disappointments with Bob's weaknesses," I told her, "until you understand how you use his weaknesses to re-experience the feelings of being abandoned, used, and deprived that you experienced with your father. You don't have to feel that way with Bob. Understand that he's the way he is not to hurt you or deprive you, but because of reasons beyond his current understanding. When you no longer react to him or try to change him, he will not feel the need to rebel against you. He will then have a chance to look at himself and his self-defeating behavior rather than spend time finding creative ways to resist you."

Sally's unhappiness had little to do with Bob and more to do with her unconscious attachment to feeling dependent on what she saw as an inconsiderate, self-absorbed person. She wanted to believe that if he could change and be the way she wanted, she could be happy. The solution to her issue with Bob depended on the degree of her emotional connection with the hurt and neglect she experienced with her father and in seeing how she transferred those same feelings onto Bob and others.

Sally worked on her issues and freed herself from feeling like a victim of Bob's unresponsive behavior. She gradually learned to accept him. Predictably, Bob improved. He began therapy and accomplished more with his job. Sally found that their relationship was far more harmonious and equal. As she said, "When I was into being a victim of Bob, I couldn't see all the ways that he was there for me or all the things that he did. I was seeing the glass half empty."

Caterers need to understand why they react so strongly to the weaknesses of others. Are those weaknesses a reflection of parts of yourself that you do not want to acknowledge? Are you replaying the same disappointments and deprivations you experienced with your parents?

The Magic Gesture

Lloyd, a businessman in his early thirties, lived on the edge of financial ruin. He had a habit of loaning money to his friends and relatives. Rarely were these loans repaid. Meanwhile, he worried about paying his bills and admitted to feeling angry about being unappreciated for the help he gave.

Unwittingly, Lloyd had set up this pattern of feeling used. On the surface, he believed his giving was an altruistic gesture. He felt appreciated and in control as long as people depended on him, though he responded with horror at the thought of being dependent on others. Being dependent made him feel powerless and helpless. He remembered having strong feelings of being withheld from and unappreciated as a child.

Lloyd was giving to others what he felt he never received from his parents. This form of giving, called a "magic gesture," was a way to be "better" than his parents who he felt never cared enough for him. The magic gesture, unfortunately, became another means to perpetuate the hurt of not being supported by them.

The magic gesture works this way in the unconscious mind: "You see, Mom and Dad, I'm far more giving and caring than you ever could be. If only you had given to me half of what I give to others. See how I respond to other people's needs— unlike you, who never responded to my needs. This is how I wanted you to treat me."

Lloyd's mother had been an alcoholic and his father had been absent a great deal. His mother made frequent requests for Lloyd's attention and time, ordering him to clean, cook, and manage the house. He took responsibility for keeping the house running smoothly, as well as managing his mother's dark moods. He reversed his feelings of being ignored and unappreciated by becoming a nurturing parent to his parents. He avoided situations of dependence on others because he believed they would let him down and disappoint him as he felt his parents had.

This pattern of giving to others what he felt he never received was repeated throughout his life, keeping alive the inner pain of emotional neglect. Not until he gained an understanding of his self-denying behavior did he stop his rescuing and make his own needs a priority.

Helping as a Form of Control

The following example of "helping" masks a subtle form of control. June, a business manager, had bought her first house, and her mother insisted on helping her unpack. Her mother's "help" consisted of telling her how to design the house, what should go where, what color would look good in the living room, and so on. Her mother "took over" and controlled the move.

Her mother took the opportunity to lecture June on her character defects, telling her, "Whatever happened to that nice man we liked? If you continue to be so picky, you'll never find a man. You need to lose 10 pounds and do something with your hair."

In the past, June had absorbed her mother's intrusiveness while seething with inner rage. She had avoided confrontation, not wanting to hurt her mother's feelings. This time June decided to speak up. "Mom, I know you just want to help me. But I want to make the decisions on how to arrange things. I also want to decide what I want for myself and my life. I'm a grown woman and it is my life. If I want advice from you about my supposed defects, I'll ask for it."

Her mother became defensive and replied, "Well, I was just trying to help, but I can see that you are being stubborn and don't want my help." She left in a huff.

June told me this incident captured the essence of their relationship. Her mother's help or control was never overtly aggressive, yet June felt she was never allowed to make her own decisions. She felt her mother wanted to take charge of her life, tell June what clothes to buy, what food to eat, what friends were okay. She experienced her mother hovering over her watching her every move. "If I looked like I was slipping, Mom would jump right in and rescue."

When June protested, her mother would say, "I'm only looking out for your welfare. I care what happens to you." June believed that her mother lived her life through her, that her mother had no identity on her own and felt worthless. She also felt her mom secretly resented her success and took any attempt by June to become independent as disrespect and rejection.

Caterers such as June's mother need to understand that unsolicited lectures on character defects or suggestions on how others should live never produce desired improvements. It is wrong to assume that people change for the better once their flaws are pointed out. The opposite often occurs: analyzing another's flaws causes him or her to dislike you and resist change.

Giving lectures to someone close to you about his character flaws is usually a result of projection, meaning you are projecting your own unrecognized character defects onto that person. June's mother accused her daughter of being too picky with men, but being picky was the mother's problem. She was picky about June's appearance and furniture arrangement, among many other things.

Feeling Betrayed When Others Refuse to Change

Many emotional caterers take personally the apparent refusal of others to change or accept their positive efforts to help. Susan, an eager young mother, tried to feed her children healthy food. She felt her own mother had showed little interest in healthy food, and Susan was determined to give her children a better start in life. One evening she painstakingly prepared an elaborate meal of fresh beet soup, tofu burgers, and fresh green salad loaded with spinach leaves. When the children sat down for dinner, their faces contorted in disgust.

"Yuck, what's that stuff? You expect us to eat this—no way."

Disappointed, she angrily replied, "Then you will have to go to bed without your supper." A war of wills ensued, with the children continuing to defy her demand to eat the beet soup and tofu burgers. In a fury, she smashed a dinner plate against the wall (no doubt a substitute for their heads) and sent them to their rooms.

Susan had personalized their rejection of her food. If they rejected her food, then they rejected her. Her rage was a protest, "You see how much I hate being rejected and unappreciated." But Susan protested too much. Her reaction indicated that she was taking their refusal personally. Looking back upon the incident, she realized the children were only asserting their independent taste buds.

Rejection and betrayal can also be experienced whenever you see your partner pursuing an interest you disapprove of. One client felt betrayed every time his overweight wife ate with gusto. "She is not doing anything to lose weight. She is doing this to torture me," he complained. "She knows how much I dislike her weight." Meanwhile, she felt the same way about his passion for beer.

Whatever others are involved in—whether food, drink, ideas, sports, TV, or hobbies of any sort—can be taken as "evidence" they are not interested in you.

You can easily interpret another person's unwillingness to change their offensive behavior as refusal to give you what you want or an indication of rejection. Jim, a businessman, felt betrayed when his alcoholic mother refused to change. He had been trying for years to get her to quit drinking. At one point, she acquiesced and set in motion plans to enter a treatment program. Jim eagerly made the arrangements, but she changed her mind and told him she no longer had a drinking problem.

His mother apparently had never intended to deal with her problems. He took personally her refusal to acknowledge her problems and felt betrayed. I asked him how it felt to see his mother stuck in this way, refusing to help herself, and unwilling to follow his advice.

"I feel that she doesn't see that I exist or consider my views and feelings," he replied. "She's so involved with herself and her issues that she's not involved with me at all. She's not sensitive to me, I am nothing to her. I also feel forced to bear the cost of her disease, to take on extra responsibility for her as I always had to do in my childhood."

"The only thing you are responsible for," I told him, "is your attachment to those feelings of being ignored, betrayed, and made to feel responsible. If you make your happiness contingent on your mother's recovery, you will likely spend the rest of your life unhappy. You will soak up the miserable feelings that you allow your mother to generate in you. You didn't create your mother's problem, nor do you have to take responsibility for it or the consequences of her problem. She didn't refuse recovery to reject you. You set yourself up to feel betrayed, helpless, and personally victimized by her inability to face herself."

Compulsive Rescuing Backfires

Compulsive rescuers are not aware that their suggestions and solutions often produce a negative reaction in the person they are trying to help. One woman became extremely angry whenever her mother tried to "help" her. "When I share with mother my feelings about my job, she takes over the conversation, gives solutions, and tries to fix my problem. She thinks I'm an imbecile who can't handle my own life. Her attempts to fix me make me feel inadequate."

People on the receiving end of unwanted sermons, recommendations, or pop therapy tend to resist the advice and may even step up their inappropriate behavior. Such "help" invites a defensive reaction, for the one being helped feels reduced and controlled by the helper. To protest against this feeling of being controlled, the one being helped often does just the opposite of what is suggested.

Because of this inner resistance to being helped, rescuers end up feeling used. They wallow in the pain of not being appreciated for their efforts. Since they are always ready to serve others, they feel emotionally deprived and abandoned when others do not reciprocate. When the one being "helped" fails to change, rescuers feel inadequate and responsible for the failure. They take the other's resistance as an indication that he or she does not respect or love them.

Compulsive rescuers are not aware that their attempts to "care" or to "help" often reinforce dependency and passivity in the one being helped. It discourages the one being "helped" from taking responsibility for himself and his stressful predicaments. The more the "helpee" receives, the more he expects to be rescued. The more he is rescued from taking responsibility for himself, the deeper his dissatisfaction and dependency can become. Consequently, he puts more pressure on helpers to take care of him. Yet, ironically, the more he is helped, the more he resents the helpers for making him aware of his passivity and dependency.

Many people secretly seek to be controlled and

directed by someone else. They want to be told what is wrong with them, how to feel, and how to conduct their lives. They are frightened by the prospect of taking charge of their lives and making their own decisions.

Unconsciously, they are not interested in working out their problems, only in getting sympathy or support. They easily fall prey to anyone who purports to have answers to their problems.

This need to be rescued or directed by others is a recreation of childhood feelings of helplessness and dependency. Most of us as children were directed in what to feel, think, and do. As adults, we transfer this expectation to be dominated over to spouses, friends, children, doctors, teachers, or bosses. Or we may have had parents who gave us little direction. Then we look for parental authority figures to give us the support and direction we did not get in the past.

Making decisions for others or telling them what is wrong with them deprives them of learning to access their own feelings, make their own decisions, and take charge of their own lives. People learn to grow and mature through their mistakes. They will never become emotionally independent without the motivation of having to make it on their own.

Emotional caterers attempt to deal with the emotional reactions that others trigger in them by giving more or "giving in." But it really makes the problem worse. Parents who rescue (emotionally or financially) their adult children can set themselves up to feel controlled and unappreciated. Parental rescuing is sometimes based on fear that without help the son or daughter will either hate them or fall apart without their intervention.

Such parents unconsciously transfer their unresolved emotional issues with their own parents onto their children. They recreate old feelings of being controlled and unappreciated by their parents by allowing their children's dependence to dominate and control them.

Some parents rescue their children in a reaction to their own childhood memories of financial hard times and deprivation. They compensate by giving their children the protection, benefits, and luxuries they were denied.

Compulsive catering to children can also be a substitute for emotional intimacy and attention. Rather than listening to their children and getting involved with their feelings, parents show "love" by giving material things.

It is every child's fantasy to get everything he or she wants without having to expend effort. A child fails to learn how to apply effort to attain what he wants when parents have given him everything on demand and rescued him from all discomfort. Often children assume they are incompetent or inadequate because their parents feel the need to rescue them. They do not learn to take responsibility or consider the consequences of their actions. They expect to be bailed out.

Under these conditions, children fail to build up a strong sense of self. Such children can lack motivation, become addictive, and depend on others or on substances. They might also develop into demanding tyrants who feel entitled to everything they desire.

Rescuers are Self-Centered

The emotional caterer is laden with the self-interest he so loudly criticizes in others. Rescuing, giving, or helping are insurance policies against anticipated rejection, disapproval, and abandonment. The rescuer secretly hopes to relieve himself of the threat of rejection in the emotional reactions of others. As one woman expressed it, "I believed that if I did what Dad wanted and pleased him, I'd prevent his angry rages. I tried so hard to win his love by jumping every time he wanted me to do something and being the kind of person he wanted."

In reaction to their own helplessness, children need to feel they have power to control their parents' threatening emotions. They believe that by being good they prevent anger and unhappiness. Rescuing becomes a way to control and manipulate other people's feelings.

Most rescuing is conditional. It says, "I'll give to you, but I secretly want you to do what I want or to be the way I want you to be." You hope that others will feel so appreciative of your giving that they will respond in an appreciative manner. As one mother told her son, "After all I've done for you, you won't even come and visit me when I'm not well. I expect you to give me some respect and caring after all I've done for you." Caterers usually cave in to this kind of emotional blackmail.

Helping can also provide a purpose and meaning for your life. Taking on the burdens and responsibilities of others gives you focus and direction. You establish your value and importance by being indispensable.

Unable to live for ourselves, we dedicate our lives to others. We see others as extensions of ourselves and need them to be like us or adopt our lifestyle so that we can feel good about ourselves. Consequently, we assume the role of zealous wardens or benevolent healers who police the private lives of our friends and families and covertly coerce others to abide by our version of proper behavior, health, and thought. We believe that what is best for us is best for everyone. Resistance to our suggestions is taken as personal rejection.

It is hard for us to see others as separate from ourselves with their own unique feelings and perspectives. We do not let others take responsibility for their lives because we do not know how to take responsibility for our lives. The emotional independence of others causes us great fear because we are afraid of our own emotional independence. How can we allow other people freedom to be themselves when we are unable to give this freedom to ourselves?

It is egocentric to believe that your words, actions, and behavior can change another person or cause his salvation. One woman made the claim, "If I visit my sister and leave my husband behind, I just know something bad will happen to him." This woman believed she had the power to keep her husband alive and that he would collapse without her. This impression represented her need to have control in order to avoid feeling powerless. The wife was encouraging her husband's dependency on her as well as reinforcing her willingness to be responsible for his life. This was a cover-up for her own feelings of dependency and helplessness if she were to lose him.

Rescuers like to feel that the good that befalls another person comes through them. A woman remarked about her husband, "He wouldn't be where he is today without me." Others fancy themselves as would-be healers, transforming the pain of others into health and wellbeing. This "power" enhances the self-worth of the caterer and gives him a feeling of power and control over his environment.

An individual does not have the power to make or cause anyone to be changed or healed. If the other person does respond positively to your suggestions, it is because he is making a choice within himself to change. The "healer" merely acts as a catalyst for the growth mechanism to kick off within another person. This is what "appropriate giving" is all about. You have a positive influence on others by "being" an example of your principles and values.

Compulsive rescuing rarely results in satisfaction for the rescuer. Because it is motivated by self-interest, it breeds disappointment and lack of appreciation. Genuine helping, however, involves no personal investment or underlying self-centered intent.

What Constitutes Healthy Helping?

Appropriate giving consists of interested and concerned detachment. Detachment is not to be confused with an "I-don't- care-anymore" attitude which is an avoidance reaction to disappointment. Many people also confuse detachment with denial and repression. But it does not mean becoming numb or unfeeling.

True detachment means you no longer feel a victim of the other person's weaknesses. You understand his point of view and have compassion for his emotional distress. You realize you cannot control the feelings or behaviors of others, and you accept them as they are without the need to change them. You do not feel blame or responsibility for the other person's problems.

The detached, compassionate person gives, when appropriate, for the feeling of pleasure in giving with no expectation in return. She gives out of choice, not out of obligation or fear. Her serenity remains intact even when others around her are miserable. Whereas the emotional caterer sacrifices her own needs, the compassionate person does not fear to reveal her needs, feelings, and boundaries. She does not fear the negative reactions of others if she does not perform according to their expectations.

Compassionate giving, therefore, has no expectations or conditions attached. There is no need to change or to modify another person's version of reality. If another person fails to respond to one's suggestions, there is no resentment. Nothing is expected from the person being helped in the way of appreciation, recognition, or acknowledgment. If the other person does not choose to respond to your help, that is his choice.

Concerned detachment means being present to the other person's problem or pain. It means listening with an open, caring attitude without needing to fix or resolve the other person's feelings. It means not carrying the emotional burden of the other person's problem or identifying with the other person's pain.

Most people simply want to be heard and understood and not given a lecture on what they should do. One client noted that every time she complained about her job to her husband, he tried to tell her what to do about it. Or he would say, "Well, why don't you quit?" His reaction was an attempt to fix or eradicate her feelings rather than to listen and accept what she was feeling. She felt dismissed and negated by his "help," which he put forward to get rid of the emotional burden he felt was imposed upon him. She merely wanted him to listen, understand, and care. He needed to be present to her, not necessarily to say anything in particular.

It takes a shift in consciousness to be a witness to another's pain without trying to solve it, as one client discovered. "I spent a good deal of time listening and supplying my parents with insight into their marriage conflicts," she said. "During one conversation, it became clear to me they were not at all interested in what I had to say. They wanted me there as a sounding board, each trying to convince me that his and her point was valid. I became aware that they really didn't seem to want to resolve their problems. No wonder they're not taking my insights seriously. It was nothing personal against me or my advice. But their lack of response to my feedback was a reflection of how trapped they were in their pain."

When this woman shifted to being a detached witness, she learned that people resolve their problems when they're ready. She also realized that their pain was not her problem. She was not a personal failure because she could not make them happy. With this understanding, she accepted her parents being stuck in their pain while she maintained an attitude of detachment that was still compassionate and caring.

The genuine helper does not do for others what they

are resistant to doing for themselves. He knows that people learn from their mistakes, and he allows others to make those mistakes. He has compassion for others but refuses to be a victim of their problems. He lets others know he respects their ability to resolve their own difficulties.

Another person's wellbeing may require that she mobilize her own resources. When a caterer takes over, she can deprive the other person of an opportunity to develop his own confidence and self-expression. The genuine helper trusts others to handle their own problems and does not anticipate being a victim of someone else's incompetence.

The most effective help is given only when requested. Refrain from imposing advice or suggestions on anyone without their permission. If someone is soliciting help, it is important to have him define clearly the kind of help or support he wants. Ask, "How can I help you with this problem?" Be honest and let the other person know if you are unable to give him what he wants.

Even when help is solicited, be aware of the motivation of the person asking for it. Is the other person looking to you because he is not taking responsibility for his own problems? Is this person holding you responsible for a decision he is afraid to make himself? Does he habitually look for someone to tell him what to do? It takes courage and confidence to allow others to struggle with their own distressful predicaments and not feel emotionally liable for their inner choices.

Do not give to others at your own expense. Genuine caring and helping do not mean sacrificing your needs or jeopardizing your own welfare. Putting yourself at risk out of a sense of duty or obligation produces resentment. You will feel unappreciated and used. If you give because you fear rejection or alienation, you are setting yourself up to feel dominated, intimidated, and emotionally exploited.

Basically, we have little capacity to change others. Change comes as a result of a person's own insights and commitment to change. No words or actions wash away another's character defects.

Rescuers need to turn their gaze inward to witness their own emotional reactions to the people around them. They need to ask themselves, "Why am I allowing myself to be so affected by this person's problems? Why do I need this person to acknowledge his weaknesses? What do I expect to gain if this person changes according to my expectations? What will I feel if this person never changes? Why is it so important to me that others respond the way I want?

You can maintain your own feelings of wellbeing no matter how miserable others are. Their unhappiness is their problem; how you allow yourself to be affected by them is your problem.

Compulsive giving indicates an unconscious attachment to being seen by others as having no value. To strive compulsively to rescue, save, enlighten, or change others also indicates an unconscious attachment to being used, controlled, and exploited.

True compassion extends the right amount of help with no expectation of return. Compassion means understanding that the other person is behaving the only way he knows how. It means witnessing the other but not feeling a victim of his behavior. With compassion, there is choice in how to respond and no feeling of obligation or guilt.

The best way to have impact on others is to become healthy yourself and manifest the values, principles, and qualities you want to see in others. When you do this, you will not need others to be any different from what they are. You are now in a position to give without emotional or personal investment in the outcome.

Exercises

- List the people you feel obligated to help, serve, please, or rescue. Describe the relationship and how you cater to them. How does it feel to be involved in this way with them? Do any images come to mind that would be a metaphor for the relationship? For example, "I feel like a puppet pulled in all directions."
- Describe what you want for the people you are rescuing. How do you want them to be? Why do you need them to be that way? Let your mind go back to childhood. Do you see any similarities with your mother, father, siblings, or relatives? How are those past relationships similar to your current relationships?
- What would you feel if you let go of your need to rescue, save or help others? Where do these feelings come from?

Chapter 8
Taking Responsibility for Others

ECS Creed:
- You are responsible for the emotional wellbeing of others. You are to blame when others are depressed, unhappy, or angry. You are responsible for how their lives turn out.
- Never allow yourself to be happy unless everyone around you is happy.
- Without your effort, nothing would get done. You have to initiate everything. You have to do it all because you do it better than anyone else. Take pride in your ability to carry the burden of other people's inadequacies.
- You cannot depend on anyone else to be as responsible or reliable as you are. You don't need anyone. Never let anyone know you are needy or vulnerable. Always maintain the image of being all-together and totally competent.

Many caterers get entangled in a form of mutual dependency in which they assume the emotional and physical responsibility for the wellbeing of others.

When you become emotionally enmeshed in the lives of others, you believe you are responsible for their unhappiness, personal inadequacies, anger, bad behavior, and pain. You believe that you, and only you, can make them feel better or become better people. You feel indispensable: without you, they would not make it.

This is the only way caterers know how to relate to others. They do not believe there is life independent of another person's painful struggles. While it feels as if the other person depends on him, a caterer really lives for the other person. His own life is diminished, and he has little in the way of independent thoughts and feelings.

Josephine revealed this emotional pattern when she said, "I feel empty. My life has no purpose. There is nothing to motivate me. I feel aimless. It's hard for me to make even the smallest decisions." She had just ended her twenty-year marriage to a man to whom she had catered, and now she was exhibiting the typical symptoms of catering "withdrawal."

Josephine believed she had no self independent of her husband. Her purpose had been to support his aspirations and needs. Taking care of her husband and her children had become her life focus.

"I've always leaned on external supports," she said. "It felt secure knowing that my husband was there to pick me up, to give me direction. Without him, I feel I don't have a safety net. No one is here to support me or reassure me. I feel like I'm out on a ledge by myself and at any moment I'll be blown away."

This overwhelming sense of vulnerability is a carryover of the vulnerability we felt as children when we were so dependent on our parents. We depended on them to handle our lives, think for us, and make our decisions. The memory of this state of vulnerable dependency remains in our psyche. Enmeshed caterers fear being abandoned because it means having to take responsibility for their lives and depend on their own internal resources to survive.

The story of Alice illustrates the power of emotional enmeshment. Everyday just before five o'clock, Alice felt the knot in her stomach tighten and tension build in her neck and shoulders. A dull headache rumbled between her temples. It was time to clash with traffic and the huge crowds that delayed her trip home. She visualized sitting in traffic, waiting through three or four stoplights at a single intersection.

"What a waste of time. It ruins my day," she lamented to herself. "These drivers have no regard for my situation." She felt angry having to accept this predicament with traffic.

"Why are you in such a hurry to get home?" I asked her.

"To make my husband's and mother-in-law's dinners. They'll be upset if I'm not there to take care of them. As a matter of fact, I hate it. I hate having to rush home after working eight hours and make their dinners. I'm furious by the time I get home. I have to do everything around the house. My husband doesn't do one-tenth the work I do. And as for my mother-in-law, well, she's just a child who needs to be taken care of. My husband shifts all the responsibility for her care over to me. He's incapable of standing up to her. Even though I offered to take her in, I resent her presence and the work I have to do for her. I feel like a slave."

No wonder Alice became tense before leaving work. Traffic was not her real problem. She displaced her emotional frustration with her husband and mother-in-law onto drivers. Drivers were not responsible for Alice's feelings. The issue was with her husband and mother-in-law who Alice felt showed no regard for her feelings.

I asked Alice what she thought would happen if she stood up to her husband and told him how she felt.

"I imagine my husband would get upset and leave me," she replied. I've always felt responsible for his feelings. I'm supposed to do everything. My needs and my feelings don't count.
I'm afraid to make my needs known to my husband. Frankly, I don't even know what my needs are."

"You are denying your needs, while focusing on the needs of others," I observed. "You put yourself through torture every evening, first feeling anxiety for failing to take care of their needs and then feeling guilt for resenting them both. But the real issue you're revealing here has more to do with setting yourself up to feel taken advantage of and neglected. You allow yourself to be controlled by their emotional reactions, and that's a cover up for your attachment to feeling emotionally abandoned and deprived."

Alice was unconsciously attached to feeling neglected and used. She was in the habit of denying her own feelings and needs and convinced she had no rights of her own. "Do these feelings of being neglected and taken advantage of remind you of your childhood?" I asked.

"It's almost an exact replica," she said. "To me, my mom was needy and fragile. I believed she would collapse if I was not there to take care of her. I felt it was my responsibility to keep Mom alive. Mom saw the world as dangerous. She never wanted me to play with other kids. I was to come straight home from school and be there for her and help her around the house. Mom would be depressed and miserable if I wasn't there. She insisted on holding my hand on the way to school until I was eleven years old. She made me wear winter clothes in summer to prevent me from catching cold. I felt responsible for Mom's misery and unhappiness. One time I was out playing with the neighbor's kids and my dad came at me in a fury. 'Why aren't you home with your mother? She needs you,' he yelled. I felt awful.

"I had to submit to Mother and take care of her. I was Mom's security blanket. She would either turn into a raving lunatic or evaporate in thin air if I didn't respond according to her wishes. I didn't have a life of my own. I was emotional 'food' for my mother. As long as I gave of myself, she could feel loved. Giving up my needs kept her alive, made her happy, and gave her strength. I was too terrified of being hated or abandoned by her to care about my needs and feelings. My value to her rested solely on

117

my ability to submit to her needs and do what she wanted. I was an extension of mother. I felt consumed and drained by her. Her love sucked out my soul."

Alice's father was verbally abusive and controlling. Her mother was unable to stand up to him and passively endured his harassment. Unconsciously, Alice identified with her mother's passivity and hurt, but she masked this feeling of vulnerability by taking care of her mother. She felt she had to make up for her mother's inability to deal with father. As an adult, she repeated this passive pattern by making up for her husband's inability to stand up to his mother.

Alice's childhood anticipation of being rejected and abandoned was transferred onto her husband and mother-in-law. Beneath the alleged superiority of being the caretaker, she recreated the subservience, self-denial, and feeling of being consumed she had experienced with her mother. Alice was accustomed to taking responsibility for other people's feelings and needs, as she learned to do with her mother. She allowed people and circumstances to make her feel the way she had with her mother—ignored, controlled, and prevented from doing what she wanted.

I had Alice draw a picture that represented this emotional pattern. She came back with a picture of herself covered with leeches. The leeches symbolized the people she felt she had to nurture and keep alive. This is how she described the picture, "I feel drained, tired, and empty. I'm not supposed to have a life of my own. There is no time for me. I get nothing from this experience. I exist only to keep these leeches alive. Without me, they would die. The only thing I get is the powerful feeling that I keep the leeches alive, that they depend on me for their life. I helplessly allow them to take my life."

What Alice really kept alive was the old feeling of being drained and starved emotionally. This feeling was so deeply woven throughout her life, binding her to moods of sadness, that she would hardly imagine a life without leeches.

Alice had held herself responsible for her mother's unhappiness. She believed that as long as mother was unhappy or miserable, she herself could not be happy. "How do you think your mother would react if you were happy and successful?" I asked Alice.

She replied, "If I'm happy and successful, I assume my mother will feel abandoned and won't like me anymore. She will assume that I don't care for her or won't be there for her. Our whole relationship is based on me rescuing her from her misery. I also feel that I won't get any attention from her if I'm happy. The only way to get her attention is to have a problem, to be sick or unhappy. Unless she is happy, I cannot be happy. Otherwise, it would end our relationship."

With this belief, Alice was destined to remain unhappy. Her unhappiness and self-denial had no effect on her mother, nor did it cure her mother's depression and unhappiness. Being overly available to her mother most likely reinforced in her mother the belief that she could get Alice's attention by being unhappy and miserable.

The belief that her mother could not be happy if Alice were happy only gave Alice license to deny herself. Alice was covering up buried feelings of being abandoned and ignored by her mother in childhood. Her mother, not Alice, had received all the attention. Alice did not feel she existed as a person in her own right, and she reversed this painful feeling of unworthiness by "being there for her mother" in ways that mother was never there for her.

Alice needed to face the hurt she repressed over her mother's lack of interest in her as a person. As long as Alice held onto the role of being a "security blanket" for others, she would continue to sacrifice her life, deny her interests, and give up her freedom.

As children, many of us felt powerless and helpless to

119

influence events. "I felt totally helpless, as if there were nothing I could do that would make any difference," Alice said of her childhood. "I had no influence on my parents. I felt dead, paralyzed, stuck. There was no movement from this position. I had to swallow whatever they dished out. No wonder I feel so lifeless."

In order to reverse these unpleasant feelings, the child creates an illusion of power by believing that he causes the emotional responses in his parents. By assuming responsibility for the parents' feelings and reactions, the child manages to sidestep the terror he feels when the people he is dependent upon are angry or distressed. The child claims power by believing he has the ability to control his parents' emotional reactions. Unfortunately, this fantasy of power exacts a big price. The child denies himself, even negates himself, so his parents can feel good about themselves.

Taking responsibility for his parents' unhappiness also allows the child to reverse the painful feeling of being a helpless victim of caretakers who do not provide for him adequately. The child blames himself for not taking care of the needs of his parents, rather than face the horrible feeling that his parents are not acknowledging him or providing for his emotional needs.

Children are not able to entertain the notion that the emotional upsets of their parents have nothing to do with them. They are convinced they are the cause for their parents being upset. Most children, for instance, believe they are responsible when parents divorce: "I, because of my badness, caused Mom or Dad to separate." In believing this, the child takes some control over inner feelings of being ignored, rejected, or powerless when his parents threaten to divorce.

Taking the Blame
Another indication of emotional catering is the

tendency to believe what others say about you and buy into false accusations made about your motives and behavior. Though you may know intellectually their accusations are false, emotionally you are willing to take the blame.

When Jenny stood up to her husband and refused to give up her night classes, her husband accused her of being a greedy, selfish person. Jenny felt crushed by his remarks and began to reconsider her decision. Being enmeshed with her husband, it felt to her that whatever he said about her had a ring of truth. Jenny soaked up the hurt and bought into his accusation that she was selfish and disloyal even though she had catered to him and given into his needs for years. Jenny had little ability to be objective or to see into her husband's motivation for berating her, which was to get her to do what he wanted.

Cassie, a 32-year-old housewife, told me about an incident with her husband who had accused her of lying about why she came home late from work. She had not lied, but she bought into the accusation and felt shamed. If she had not been so willing to be put down by him, she might have replied, "Look, John, I know I didn't lie. I refuse to take responsibility for something I didn't do. Obviously, you are having some kind of negative reaction to this situation. Can you tell me why you are reacting like this?"

Why are we so eager to take the blame? Children tend to believe their parents are always right, and they instinctively feel belittled or at fault when accusations are leveled against them. Sometimes children only get attention when they are being lectured, blamed, or accused of some wrongdoing. Parents often release their own frustrations by picking on their children. A child receives the message, "There's something wrong with me." As I mentioned, taking the blame and bearing the responsibility for someone else's unhappiness is a way to reverse underlying feelings of powerlessness. Taking the blame gives us the illusion of having control.

For this reason, caterers adopt the following attitude: "If something is wrong, it's my fault." Whatever goes wrong, caterers jump right in and assume the blame. Here's a few examples:

- If my husband is unhappy at the party, it's my fault.
- If the business I work for fails, it's my fault.
- If my wife isn't satisfied with the furniture, it's my fault.
- If a hurricane hits and wrecks our house, it's a sign of my disfavor with God.
- If my children can't budget their money properly, it's my fault.
- If my children fail, it's my fault.
- If my husband's in a rage, it's my fault.
- If a friend is depressed, it's my fault and my responsibility to fix it.

Take a moment and reflect on all the situations or people you feel responsible for. How does it feel to be so responsible, to take the blame for everything? Do you feel a sense of responsibility for yourself? Who takes responsibility for your feelings and needs?

The Guilt Trip

Caterers readily assume guilt whenever someone close to them is upset with them. Rosemarie, a legal secretary with two children, spoke with annoyance about her mother's constant demand for attention. If Rosemarie did not phone her at least every second day, her mother was on the phone wondering what had happened, subtly accusing Rosemarie of neglecting her. Rosemarie felt guilty for resenting her mother's demands and intrusions. Each week something new was required: taking her to the doctor, dealing with her accountant, moving her furniture into storage, or spending hours entertaining her. When mother beckoned, she jumped.

"How do you feel when your mother makes requests for your time?" I asked.

"I feel I have to drop whatever I'm doing and take care of her. I feel obligated to her. I also feel oppressed and drained."

"What if you should refuse to act as a 'satisfaction machine' for your mother? What do you imagine would happen?"

"She would lay a big guilt trip on me. She would accuse me of being selfish, mean, and neglectful. I'd be blamed for her unhappiness, criticized as an unloving daughter. She'd hate me and never want to speak to me again."

Rosemarie had given up her autonomy and needs in order to feel loved and cherished. Allowing herself to be emotionally blackmailed (the guilt trip) by her mother, she ended up entangled in feeling deprived and emotionally neglected. She bought into the belief that she was selfish for not responding to her mother's every need. This belief covered up her unconscious attachment to feeling criticized, rejected, and abandoned by her mother. Rosemarie unknowingly perpetuated the pain of being up against someone who ignored her and who was insensitive to her needs.

Rosemarie's mother believed her daughter should be instantly available to satisfy her every demand. Rosemarie had been playing into this game of parenting her, thereby validating her mother's demands and intrusions, leaving Rosemarie feeling more deprived, neglected, and controlled.

Two months later, she told me of an incident with her mother that ended very differently. During the family dinner, her mother had telephoned angry and drunk. Her mother was having a fight with her father, and she had

123

called Rosemarie expecting her to come over and resolve their problem. In the past, Rosemarie would have dropped everything and ran to their aid. This time she told her mother, "I'm no longer going to pay the price for your drinking or your problems with Dad. This time, Mother, you'll have to solve this problem on your own."

Rosemarie felt good about standing up to her mother, but she still had guilt and fear that her mother would never speak to her again. But these fears were unwarranted. Her mother did resolve her own problem that night, and stopped calling Rosemarie when such circumstances arose. As Rosemarie established new boundaries with her mother, they developed a new closeness. Her mother learned to take responsibility for her problems with her marriage, rather than relying on Rosemarie to rescue her.

Rosemarie had fallen for the childish plea of her mother, "If you really love me, you'd be here for me when I need you." She accepted the accusation that she would be selfish and unloving not to respond. Her alleged crime of selfishness covered up her attachment to feeling controlled and deprived of her own needs and interests. By sacrificing herself to serve her mother, and making her mother's problems her own, she secretly maintained feelings of being used and emotionally abandoned.

I told Rosemarie, "As a child, you felt you had no option other than to comply with your mother's needs. The problem is you still react to others as a child, expecting they will reject or abandon you if you do not sacrifice for them. You cannot be held responsible for how you reacted as a child, but you are responsible for how you react today. The good news is that you no longer have to indulge in being abandoned or let down if you let others handle their own problems."

Helping Others at Your Own Expense

Many readers will relate to this following example. Jill and Marie were close friends. At lunch one day, Jill told Marie her apartment lease would expire in two weeks, and she had not yet found another apartment. Marie felt subtle pressure to let Jill move in to her apartment, though she did not really want Jill to stay with her. But she blurted out, "Why don't you stay with me until you find other arrangements."

Later, Marie awoke in the middle of the night feeling irritated. She had felt compelled to rescue Jill even though Jill had not even made a direct request. This was Marie's pattern— to say *yes* to situations she later regretted.

Marie felt that if she had not made the offer, Jill would not like her, would see her as selfish for having a large apartment to herself, and would end their relationship. Marie also began to see how obligated she felt to please other friends and take care of their needs.

"I do this in every aspect of my life," Marie explained. "I'm never honest with myself or with others. I put myself at their disposal, and then I get angry and resent them for it. Then I isolate myself so I won't be taken advantage of. But I know that's not the answer."

Marie called Jill and shared with her what she learned about her pattern of rescuing. Jill was not upset with Marie, and two days later she found suitable arrangements on her own. Marie's fear had been irrational and came from childhood fears of parental rejection had she not been compliant and giving.

In a similar situation, Joanne reluctantly agreed to watch her son's two dogs while he vacationed. She really did not want to do it but was in the habit of taking care of others, especially her children. She felt concerned they would not like her if she did not comply. But her compliance turned out to be a nightmare.

The dogs gnawed on her sofas, chairs, and shoes. They barked and kept Joanne and her husband up at night. They soiled her white carpet. She had to take them for frequent walks. By the time her son returned from vacation, she had fantasies of killing the dogs. She was furious and exhausted.

She saw from this experience how she set herself up to be a victim of her attachment to being disliked and to cater to others while putting her own needs and feelings last. Her entanglement with the dogs demonstrated the depth of her self-denial and how much it cost her.

Caterers allow themselves to be pushed around and taken advantage of. They believe they have to inhibit their honest feelings and submit to others because speaking the truth or saying *no* causes others to be angry or hurt. Their favorite phrase is, "I don't want to hurt his feelings." This expectation of hurting others regulates the caterer's words, feelings, and responses, and it puts her at the mercy of the other person's emotional reactions.

One woman told me of her issue with phone solicitors. "Years ago, when I took calls from phone solicitors, I automatically gave in and bought whatever they were selling. I just couldn't say *no*. I didn't want to be rude and hurt their feelings. Then I began to avoid answering the phone at night, or I would say, 'I'm sorry, we're eating right now,' to get them off my back. Now I just tell them 'I'm sorry but I'm not interested.' It's amazing how long it took me to be honest and direct."

Not wanting to hurt others also covers up a sensitivity to feeling hurt and criticized by others. The belief that your words can hurt hides your own expectation of being devastated by insensitive words.

Caterers often believe the behavior of another person reflects on them. If the person you are enmeshed with performs badly or appears inadequate, you believe it reflects your own inadequacies. You give the other person the power to make you look bad. This is one reason why you spend so much time and energy reforming others. Harry considered leaving his wife because of her weight problem. He felt that her inability to lose weight was a sign of weakness and a lack of will. Her weight problem made him feel that others would see him as not good enough to attract a beautiful wife. If she looked bad in the eyes of others, then he too looked bad. Harry held himself responsible for her inadequacies, as though her faults were his and she were an extension of himself.

Being enmeshed means not knowing how to set boundaries or limits with others. People who are enmeshed have little ability to recognize personal boundaries and allow others to intrude into their lives. They also reserve the right to intrude into other people's lives. Not having a solid sense of themselves, they do not know where they begin and where the other person leaves off. They do not know how to relate or interact with others without fixing problems or sharing pain.

Why Do I Have to Do It All?

Another role of emotional catering is the super-responsible hero. These people hide their inner wounds of feeling neglected by becoming all things to all people and juggling multiple roles and responsibilities. They carry the responsibility for financial security, household chores, family problems, job conflicts, as well as emotional wounds. They are competent, self-sufficient achievers who have a habit of getting entangled with needy, dependent people.

If you are a super-responsible hero, you probably come across as calm, confident, and competent. You rarely express neediness. Your emotions are under control. You feel you can take care of yourself. In fact, you believe the only good you get comes from yourself. Nothing good comes from others. You take pride in feeling self-sufficient. You like being in the position of the giver, the one who takes responsibility for everything.

Why? Because you fear being dependent on others. You are convinced that being dependent means being let down and disappointed. Underneath that calm, superior exterior is a person who needs affection, nurturing, and attention. But you deny these needs and your inner feelings of worthlessness by exaggerating your competence and inflating your abilities. Your brand of self-sufficiency masks the hurt of feeling neglected and unappreciated.

As a super-responsible hero, you do not believe it possible to have a nurturing relationship. You believe independence means not being dependent on others. But in pushing others away and repressing your needs, you set yourself up for neglect and isolation. Your behaviors result from feeling overwhelmed and frightened by you own vulnerability and need to be cared for.

Being a super-responsible hero is a potent way to deny and neglect yourself. As a hero, you tend to exhaust yourself physically and emotionally. You worry about not getting things done and feel distressed if chores are not accomplished. While you run around, plugging up holes in the dike, you hear an inner voice complaining, "Why do I always have to be responsible around here and take on all the burdens?"

Inwardly you gloat, "Unlike others who are irresponsible, I can always be counted upon to complete a task." But a river of bitterness drowns real satisfaction "If only others would go to such lengths as I do," you complain. "No one goes out of their way like this for me." Yet you suffer in silence and compensate for the unfairness and lack of appreciation by feeling superior.

As a pseudo-hero, you must appear strong and all-together. You maintain this image by arranging your life to please others, making sure they see you in the best possible light. You avoid situations where you might receive help from others since receiving feels uncomfortable. In your eyes, people who need help are weak and inadequate, which reflects your inner conviction about yourself.

"Why see a therapist?" the pseudo-hero retorts. "They don't know anything I don't know. Besides, they really don't know what they're doing. They haven't even got their own acts together."

You do not expect to get anything of value from doctors, therapists, parents, friends, or spouses. This attitude goes back to your adolescence: "Mom or Dad can't tell me anything I don't already know. Besides, what do they know anyhow, they're stupid. They never gave me anything of real value. I'll take care of myself, make my own mistakes, and come to my own conclusions (even if this should cost me dearly). I'll work out my own problems, for nothing of value can come from anyone except myself."

Authority figures are especially not trusted. In your mind, they are not caring. Their sole motive is to control and take advantage of you (as you felt your parents did). Paradoxically, you tend to put trust in charlatans, stock brokers, psychics, or gurus. By trusting inappropriate people, you repeat the experience of being passively dependent on someone (such as a parent) who lets you down or controls your fate. You trust those who cannot be trusted but not those who are trustworthy.

The super-responsible hero manages to find a way to bear the burdens and responsibilities of those with whom he becomes involved. The story of Ralph illustrates how this occurs.

Ralph, at 48, owned a 200-employee business. But after many years of success, he felt weighed down by burdens and responsibilities. Besides taking care of the emotional problems of his employees, he felt pressure

129

from his wife and children to provide the financial support they expected.

"I feel as though the whole world depends on me," he remarked. "Every time I turn around, someone is in an emotional stew. It's my job to smooth things over, make it work and fix it. I'm fighting emotional fires every day of my life."

Ralph was physically exhausted and didn't sleep well. He had no time for his interests or hobbies and lost his enthusiasm for sex. He felt apathetic, isolated, disconnected from his needs and feelings, and irritated over little things. Absorbed in taking care of others, he forgot to take care of himself.

When his business slipped because of the recession, he believed it was his fault. "It's my responsibility to keep it all going," he grumbled. "These people depend on me. Now my wife wants to redecorate the house. She's never satisfied. She's always pressuring me for more money for trips, clothing, or the house. My kids need cars, college tuition, and medical treatment. Last week I got a call from my sister saying that my mother is sick and needs to be in a nursing home. Somehow it's my responsibility to take care of this problem."

"What would happen if you relinquished your sense of obligation and shut down your catering business?" I asked Ralph.

"Everyone would hate me and desert me. They would look down on me and see me as selfish. I'd feel reduced, inferior. Besides, everything would end up in total chaos. I have to be there to make sure everything goes smoothly."

Ralph's childhood was stormy and traumatic. He had a physically and verbally abusive father and a passive, doting mother. His parents were in constant conflict, and Ralph felt responsible for the abuse he saw in his parents' relationship. To deal with the terror of seeing his mother abused, he reversed his feelings of powerlessness by believing he caused the abuse to happen to her. He believed he "allowed" his mother to be verbally abused by his father. To assuage his guilt for his alleged crime, he felt responsible for protecting his mother and a need to minimize the conflict between her and his father.

Ralph had slipped emotionally into his mother's body (identified with her), and he felt indirectly that he too was being abused. To reverse this unpleasant feeling of being beaten down, he claimed power by believing that his weakness or negligence caused his mother's abuse. This alleged crime came under attack from his conscience, and he defended against this accusation by jumping to his mother's rescue. "I am not identifying with mother's abuse," his defense contended. "See how I want to quiet down Dad and make everyone happy." He rescued Mom to prove he was not a passive wimp who let Dad abuse her.

Ralph also felt hurt that his mother hadn't supported him when his father abused him. "I had to handle Dad's abuse on my own," he remembered. "I got no protection from anyone. My mother deserted me in my time of need."

Ralph's behavior showed aspects of the magic gesture. "See how I listen and resolve problems," this defense contended. "See how I take care of others and never let them down. I would never desert others in their time of need. If only you, Father and Mother, had resolved your own problems and given me one-tenth of the nurturing I give to others."

Ralph's super-responsible facade hid his secret addiction to being let down by his parents and wounded by their lack of support. It hid the bittersweet hurt of having been emotionally abandoned and neglected. Like his mother, however, Ralph played out his passivity by allowing others to take advantage of him emotionally. He did not stand up to the needy people in his life and get

131

them to take responsibility for themselves.

Barbara was another super-responsible hero who took on her family's burdens at a cost to herself.

"I've had it up to my ears," Barbara fumed. "I don't know what to do with Paul. I've been taking on the financial burdens and responsibility of the family for years now. I'm so angry and hurt. I simply can't get him to understand how I feel. I don't know whether to leave him. I'm really at my wit's end." "Tell me about your relationship with Paul," I asked.

"I've been a nurse for twelve years and have been primarily responsible for the financial and emotional support of our family. I've put in many hours working overtime just to make ends meet. I've got an ulcer and my health is poor. Paul is a musician who plays gigs a few evenings a week. He also fancies himself a songwriter who will someday make it big. Since we've been married he's played his music and written songs but never made sufficient money to support the family on his own. I make three times what he makes.

"I've tried to get him to supplement his income by doing other kinds of work, but he refuses. He says music is his life, that he loves his work and will not compromise his talent by working in some stupid low-paying job. 'Any day now,' he says, 'I'm going to make it big. Don't you know I'm doing this to help you out and support the kids!'

"What should I do?" Barbara moaned. "He says I'm a workaholic and that it's unfair of me to expect him to work like I do. So I do it all, while he sits there like a slug and expects me to clean and pick up after him. I can't depend on him for anything. It's simply not fair. I don't have the time to do what I really want. Why should he get to do what he wants and not have to worry about anything? Now I wonder, should I leave him?"

"Whether or not to leave Paul is not the point right now," I replied. "You may decide to stay with him, accepting his limitations without feeling personally hurt and victimized. Or you can draw limits with Paul and insist that he take realistic financial responsibility for the family. The way to resolve this problem is to understand how you allow yourself to feel burdened and responsible, thereby reinforcing Paul's dependency on you. It's also important for you to understand that Paul's lack of responsiveness is not an indication he doesn't love you. His dependency is a problem he must face in himself," I explained to her.

Unconsciously, Barbara was recreating her parents' marriage. Like Barbara, her mother had been involved with a self-absorbed man who was demanding and critical, with no tolerance for frustration. He shifted from job to job, never making enough money to support his family, while Barbara's mother had to work and hold down two jobs. A pleasant, friendly man on the outside, Barbara's father saw himself as a misunderstood victim whose behavior elicited pity. "I wish someone would give me a break," he often lamented. He became depressed when her mother criticized him.

Her mother stoically endured his weakness and lack of ambition. "Well, what can you or I do about it?" she often said to Barbara. Her mother complained incessantly about her husband's faults yet refused to leave him.

Barbara felt taken for granted, ignored, and unloved in her relationship with her parents. She did not feel her parents responded to her needs, nor saw her as a person in her own right. She felt forced to take care of what she perceived as incompetent, irresponsible parents who blamed her for not doing enough. To hide the hurt of feeling emotionally abandoned and unloved, she nurtured one person after another and recreated in her marriage with Paul the same hurt of feeling exploited and neglected.

"Remember that Paul and his dependency problem are not the causes of your feelings," I told her. "Like your

133

mother, you also believe that you have no options but to grin and bear it. If this emotional pattern is not resolved within yourself, you could find yourself in a similar situation again. If you work through your emotional issues with Paul, eventually you will come to a decision about the relationship. Leaving Paul at this point would merely be a phony protest covering up your own unconscious willingness to be in this kind of exploitive predicament."

Both Barbara and Paul were able to resolve their emotional issues through therapy. Barbara let go of feeling a victim of Paul's resistance to supporting the family, and Paul worked out his dependency and feelings of being deprived and controlled. He eventually understood she was not taking away his ambitions and forcing him to submit. Barbara could see that Paul loved her despite his problems.

Barbara consciously claimed she wanted support and less responsibility. Yet she managed her life so as to be free of reliance on anyone. She also saw how she did things before others got a chance, making the burden fall on her shoulders. She had taken the reality of Paul's dependency problem as a license to feel controlled by his passive neediness. She willingly took on the burden of his lack of involvement and used it to feel neglected and unloved. She also admitted feeling uncomfortable being given to and taken care of, and remembered examples of how she had resisted being helped.

When you project to others the image of a strong competent person without needs, how can you expect to receive nurturing or help? You set it up so you do not "get" from others. No one can take advantage of you without your cooperation or participation. Remember, you are the one taking on the responsibility and burdens of others.

Caterers such as Barbara feel their value rests on their acute sense of responsibility and how much they accomplish. Unconsciously, they anticipate disapproval and indifference for their efforts. Even when praise and acknowledgment are forthcoming, they feel uncomfortable with it and find ways to diminish their accomplishments.

The discrepancy between the provider and the "dependee" can eat away at the core of a relationship. The provider feels stuck in the position of "I have to do it all myself without any help," while the dependee feels, "I don't get enough help when I need it." If the dependee is kicked out and abandoned, that is taken by him as proof that the provider never helped or gave enough. The provider plays victim by paying the price for someone else's deficiencies and gets to bear the emotional responsibility of others.

Believing that your happiness causes others to reject you serves as a justification for short-changing yourself and your life. Holding yourself back or feeling bad for the unhappiness of others does not help others feel better. They are not even aware of your sacrifice. Your feelings of being deprived and ignored are the result of your own self-defeating interpretations of what you think others are feeling. Once you see how you use the way other people respond to deprive yourself of happiness, you can let others be unhappy and still maintain your own happiness.

When we take responsibility for someone else's happiness, we forfeit rights to our own happiness. Who is responsible for your happiness? When you learn to take responsibility for your own feelings and behaviors, you will have no problem letting others take responsibility for theirs. The key is observing and understanding your own feelings, reactions, and motives.

Exercises

- Write down examples of how you shoulder burdens and take on responsibility for other people's problems.

- List the people in your life who bring out in you the tendency to sacrifice yourself and your needs. Ask yourself, what would happen if you let go of the burden of their wellbeing. How does your sacrifice help them?
- Draw a picture that would symbolize the pattern of taking on the responsibility for others and doing it all.
- Ask yourself what would happen if you stopped playing the super-responsible hero.

* List all the things you were blamed for as a child. Do you still feel blamed for similar infractions in your present relationships?

* Write out the ways you believed you made your mom or dad happy as a child. Do you still act out these same behaviors with your partner or with others?

Chapter 9
The Quest for Approval

ECS Creed:
* Take any disagreement or complaint on the part of others as disapproval and a personal devaluation of yourself.
* Expect others to put you down, judge you as no good, and see you as bad or inadequate.
* Disqualify and discount any praise or positive attention.
* Belabor and draw lots of attention to your mistakes and inadequacies; justify them as best you can.
* Become obsessed with achievement and becoming perfect. Mediocrity is a capital offense worthy of great shame. Worry daily on whether or not you are measuring up.
* Expect to fail so you can look bad and incompetent in everyone's eyes.
* Torture yourself with the conviction that you will never be recognized for your talents or for who you are.

Clod— *1) A lump or mass of earth; 2) a dull stupid person; 3) blockhead, dolt, dunce, dummy.*

"That's how I feel about myself," wrote Terry, a mother and career woman. "I feel as if I am a big dirt clod. If someone picked me up and threw me, I would hit something and shatter into worthless dust. If someone were to step on me, I would be ground into the street, and no one would know I was even gone. If I were laying in a lawn, I would disappear with the first cloudburst.

"I have lived for forty-four years, pretending to have a

life when, in fact, I only take up space. I lay here and get run over as people drive by on their way through real life. I lay here and hope I don't get stepped on and crushed into absolute nothingness.

"I want to find life inside me, inside this clod, this mass of nothing. I want to find meaning and goodness inside this dummy. There must be something inside me that's more than insignificant emptiness. There has to be a germ, a bud, a beginning of something. I'm ready for my life to happen."

Terry had buried these negative feelings about herself under a superficial optimistic facade. Most caterers, whether conscious of it or not, have deep feelings of being insignificant. They feel they have no value if they are not servicing the needs and expectations of others. Their worthiness, they believe, is measured by how much they give to others and how pleased others are with them. They are convinced they will be rejected or abandoned if they do not "please" others. This pattern is a replay of their parent-child relationship.

Caterers live in anxiety and fear that someone will discover their "secret flaw," some alleged, horrible sin. "I often feel that if people got to know the real me," Terry remarked, "they would find out I am horrible and disgusting." She did not believe she could be loved for being herself.

What Causes Low Self-Esteem?

How do competent, creative people develop such a lowly opinion of themselves? This sense of inadequacy and unworthiness is a reaction to the rejection and disapproval the child "perceived" from family members. The child tries to make sense of the real or imagined rejection by deducing that it must be some innate badness within herself that caused the disapproval. The assumption of being "flawed" gives the child a feeling of power and control over her parents' disapproving responses. The child takes her parents' reactions personally and believes she causes her parents to reject or disapprove of her. Most children interpret even minor scolding for misbehavior as rejection of themselves. This is because they tend to identify themselves with their actions.

The child's conviction that his caretakers disapproved of him or rejected him, followed by the belief that some form of innate inadequacy "caused" the rejection, is the root cause of the low self-esteem cycle. The child's self-centered conviction that the world revolves around him and that others are perpetually looking down on him and his "inadequacies" persists into adulthood.

Low self-esteem really means self-centeredness. It is a remnant of the child's self-centered perspectives of reality. All children see the world as revolving around them, as if the world is preoccupied with who they are and what they are doing. Children can never get enough attention. Being self-centered means believing the focus is on yourself and how others see you.

As the child grows up, he becomes attached to the notion that other people are focused on him and are judging him negatively. He develops a "need" to feel disapproved of or invalidated by others. As a consequence of his interest in being seen in a bad light by others, he relishes any form of imagined or real criticism of his behavior or performance. To camouflage this painful attachment, he dredges up a litany of faults or imperfections such as "I'm stupid, I'm too fat and ugly," or "I just don't have what it takes." Now he can feel that he "caused" the perceived negative reaction from others.

The Power of Shame

Several years ago, I had a revealing dream that helps explain this attachment to being seen in a negative light. I was being led into a huge auditorium filled with negative, jeering people. I was naked and bound up with ropes. I was brought before the crowd because I had committed some wicked crime. I felt an overwhelming sense of shame and humiliation. The crowd jeered at me with hate and called me names. As they filed out of the auditorium, they spit at me. One face stood out from the crowd as it passed by me. It was my father's face, sneering at me, hating me, showing disgust of me.

My dream symbolized my inner attachment to being shamed and ridiculed. That shame represented my experience with my father, and how I had perceived he felt about me.

When my father told me to do a chore, he watched over my shoulder to see that I did it right. If I did not perform to his exacting standards, he became disgusted and yelled, "My God, can't you do anything right! You act like a total idiot!" If he found me relaxing or reading a book, he shouted, "Get off your lazy ass and get to work!" I remember feeling stupid, worthless, and incompetent. It seemed to me that he was always critical of me, that I never measured up. I don't remember positive praise or acknowledgment, only my father's withering looks and how I braced myself for his negative judgment.

While striving hard as an adult to be successful and win approval, I unconsciously watched for criticism and devaluation. I also pounced on my own imperfections and berated myself for not performing perfectly. I rarely felt satisfied with myself or the level of recognition I received. In my mind, my skills or talents were never appreciated or acknowledged. I felt taken for granted, used, and dismissed as no one special.

As an adult, I became afraid to compete or try new things. If I could not perform perfectly, I would not do it at all. I lived in fear that I would be looked down upon by others as inadequate and inferior. I felt shame about myself and feared that no matter what I did, I would be ridiculed and criticized. I deprived myself of success because I believed people would discover I was really a fake.

I subjected myself to the same critical treatment that my father had dished out to me. He remained active in my mind reminding me daily how bad I was doing. Consequently, I was not at all comfortable with praise. Disapproval and I had become close buddies. I remember times when I felt a vague sense of disappointment after not getting expected criticism.

I also discovered that I subjected others to the same critical treatment my father dished out to me. Unknowingly, I acted just like my father and became irritated at people who did not try to be perfect. I often obsessed over other people's flaws and shortcomings.

"Why am I always the one who has to make up for their mistakes?" I asked myself. "Why can't they do things the way I do them?" By becoming a critical authority figure, I tried to avoid feeling the victim of a critical authority figure. Unconsciously, however, I identified with the rejection and disapproval that I imagined others experienced when I criticized them. This way I indulged vicariously in being judged negatively.

As an adult, I expected others to look down on me in the same way my father had. I avoided expressing myself creatively out of fear I would be seen as foolish or inadequate. As I realized how I subjected myself to what I endured with my father and understood my addiction to disapproval, I gradually overcame my conviction of impending shame and criticism. I was able to enjoy having others interested in what I felt and who I was.

The Great Report Card in the Sky

In a desperate attempt to disguise and mask "secret flaws," caterers set up the Department of Good Impressions. By presenting a good impression, they try to

141

ward off expected shame and rejection and deny the existence of the "bad" person inside. This alleged "badness" is a fantasy created to mask their secret attachment to being seen and looked down upon by others as "losers."

As I have said, harboring hidden flaws represents an attempt to take control over the rejection and disapproval you believe will happen. The defense contends: "I, being so badly flawed, ugly and stupid, cause others to look down on me." Hence, you update your flaws as you dwell on the bad things you did to cause the real or imagined rejection. Now you will feel guilty for these alleged character flaws.

As caterers, our lives revolve around evaluation—of ourselves, of others, and of how others evaluate us. With condemnation right around the corner, we live with the anxiety of being seen as worthless failures. Every action and every decision are fraught with the prospect of being negatively judged as inadequate, wrong, or bad. When we give others the power to validate our worthiness, we give them the power to control our lives.

Another creative way to feel inferior is to compare ourselves with others. We size ourselves up as either inferior or superior. Others have more status, more intelligence, more money, a better reputation, more beauty, more popularity, or more luck. The assumption is: if others look good, we look bad. "How come you're not as successful or thin as they are? You're a real loser," the inner voice proclaims.

A friend of mine constantly compared her physical attributes to others and always came up short. She felt defective because she was not thin and attractive. She had believed her sister won more approval from her parents. Consequently, she created opportunities as an adult to feel beaten out by women she perceived to be more attractive and talented.

How we see others reflects how we see ourselves. One client saw those around her as "unpolished and unprofessional." This was exactly how she anticipated others would judge her. Unfortunately, most caterers only feel good about themselves when they feel better than someone else.

To justify our secret indulgence in being seen as losers, we minimize our skills and talents and engage in litanies of negative self-reproach. Here are a few favorites: "Why did you do that? That was stupid! You really expect to fail, don't you! You're fat and ugly and who would want you anyhow? You can't do anything right. You don't want anything good in your life. Look at yourself, what have you done with your life? How many times have you screwed things up? You'll never get what you want, you slob!" The inner jury always finds you guilty.

To defend against these inner accusations, we produce justifications or excuses such as, "The problem is that I'm a few pounds overweight. I just need to lose a few pounds." Or, "I haven't had the right breaks." Or, "I just need the proper guidance and then I'd do something with my life." Or, "It's Mom and Dad's fault. They never gave me confidence. That's my problem."

In our unconscious quest for rejection and disapproval, we scan the environment with inner antennas. We are quick to feel insulted or hurt and to interpret other people's comments or actions as against us, even when nothing of the sort was intended. We react defensively at the slightest hint we are less than perfect. We will even unconsciously provoke and elicit disapproval. Here are some common ways we can do it.

- Throw temper tantrums. Yell, scream, and fling insults at others.
- Act stupid and make dumb mistakes.
- Butt into other people's lives.

- Act like a superior know-it-all: "I don't have any problems. I don't need that kind of help. I'm already self-actualized."
- Pursue people who are not interested in you.
- Seek attention from others at inappropriate times, such as when your partner is tired and sleepy.
- Become overweight.
- Become addicted to alcohol or drugs. Such behavior invites others to lose respect for you.
- Fail in everything you do.
- Resist doing what others have requested.
- Complain and dump your problems on others.
- Act needy with others. Seek reassurance that they care for you.
- Believe that everyone hates you.

Sarah, in a treatment program for bulimia, had a knack for eliciting disapproval. She entered my office in considerable anxiety and said, "I just can't handle my life. I'm failing at my job, I just don't know what I'm doing there. Everything I do turns to mush. I guess my parents are right, I can't handle myself."

That week, on the day of the final exam for a business course she was taking, her parents had invited her to lunch. She had not wanted to go because of studying. She was sure they would be upset if she put her needs first.

Sarah went to lunch but seethed and grumbled fiercely to herself at every delay. She was upset and felt the luncheon date would cause her to fail her test. She went home and purged her lunch, then felt shame for this behavior and chastised herself. Sarah was sure this relapse meant she had failed treatment. However, she was not aware at the time how much her sensitivity to her parents' disapproval had prompted this relapse.

Sarah came from a well-to-do family with a domineering father and a passive, accommodating mother. Her father made all the decisions for his daughter and provided materially whatever she wanted. She was sheltered and protected. Once when Sarah tried to stand up for what she wanted, she was told by her mother, "I really think that what Dad and I have planned for you will be much better."

Sarah described her terror when her father cut her up with his disapproving looks and cynical comments. She felt he saw her as weak and unmotivated. Yet her life now consisted of episodes of failure, validating her father's expectations.

Her mother rescued her whenever Sarah got into a jam. She gave Sarah money and offered to intercede on her behalf with her father. She could not stand to see Sarah unhappy or disappointed and tried to do whatever she thought would make her feel good. Her mother worried intensely about Sarah's problems and how to solve them. She gave suggestions, advice, and help, which were disguised attempts at controlling Sarah. Without being aware of it, she reinforced Sarah's already entrenched view of herself as incompetent.

Actually, Sarah was quite intelligent, competent, and skilled. But as soon as she began to do well and accomplish goals, she sabotaged herself by bingeing on food and alcohol. She led a secret life of food binges and purges and alcoholic binges and abstinences. She alternated between uncontrollable indulgences and rigidly enforced starvation. Whenever she acted out, she felt a surge of power and control followed by guilt and shame. "What if someone finds out," she said fearfully. "I live in terror of someone finding out how bad I really am and feeling so shamed and disgraced."

But she was unconsciously setting herself up to be shamed.

By acting out with food and alcohol, and losing control of these substances, she proved that she was out of control

145

with her life, and she justified her father's view of her. Sarah talked about making lots of money on her own and being successful to prove to her Dad how strong and capable she really was. Yet she set up her life to fail and incur her Dad's negative judgments.

Please Don't Take this Personally

Perhaps nothing causes more unhappiness than taking personally other people's comments, reactions, unhappiness, or feedback. Sue and Bill's marriage illustrated this problem.

Sue had been married to Bill for thirty years. He was demanding and expected her to agree with him and tolerate his abusive, demeaning comments. He often raged at her whenever she was assertive enough to challenge his ideas or behaviors. He attacked her character and behavior and had no qualms resorting to vicious name-calling when he felt she disapproved of his behavior. He treated other family members with similar disrespect and eventually drove them away. Sue had tried for years to calm him down and smooth things over with the relatives. She soaked up his verbal abuse and spent hours crying over the hurt.

"How does it feel to be married to him," I asked her.

"I've gone through my entire marriage," she replied, "feeling like a slug about to be squashed. I have to listen to his critical rages and not say a word. If I don't agree with him, he flies into a rage. I don't dare challenge him. If I say anything, he will deny it, twist it around and make it all my fault. It's dangerous to speak up. I know he won't hurt me physically, but I feel as though he will if I say anything critical to him."

Sue had experienced comparable emotional terrorism in her childhood. Her father was an unhappy, angry man who had raged at everyone when things did not go his way. He was critical, demanding, and he expected Sue and her mother to serve him like slaves. Sue could not remember any praise from him, or positive acknowledgment of her accomplishments. She lived in fear of his anger. She felt she was not allowed to think for herself or have any regard for herself. Not only did she passively submit to verbal abuse from him, but she was expected to accept and approve of his behavior as well.

She became comfortably familiar with this kind of mistreatment. Unconsciously, she had chosen a man similar to her father, and she thereby subjected herself to similar abuse. Sue had become addicted to being demeaned and criticized. She rationalized her acceptance of the abuse by claiming, "I don't want to enrage him by speaking up." This excuse kept her addiction to being put down and verbally abused well-hidden.

Accustomed to being silenced, Sue silenced herself, as well as her feelings and her creative aspirations. She criticized herself in the same manner that her father and husband reproached her. By allowing herself to be mistreated by her husband, she doomed herself to a life of hurt and loneliness and kept alive the same feelings she had experienced as a child.

As Sue began to connect with her addiction to being demeaned and mistreated, she gained the courage to speak up and challenge Bill. At first, he was incensed by her new-found confidence. But when he realized she was no longer afraid of his outbursts, he began to take a look at his own behavior.

Like Sue, he also had a deep emotional interest in being criticized and rejected. But his defense was different. Bill took any form of disagreement or challenge from others as criticism and rejection. He then protested, trying to convince himself, "Not true I am looking to be criticized. See how much I hate it."

When others disagreed with him, Bill felt as if he were being accused of being wrong and stupid. This extreme defensiveness indicated an attachment to feeling unimportant and unworthy. Bill scanned his environment looking for any morsel of evidence that he was being criticized. He had a hard time in his relationships with others because his abrasive manner gave him what he secretly wanted—abandonment and rejection.

Bill became like his father in his marriage and subjected Sue to what he had experienced as a child. His father had berated and silenced him in the same manner that Bill silenced and berated Sue. To block out the hurt of having been oppressed and discounted, Bill became the oppressor. He began to connect with his childhood hurt of having been rejected and demeaned and saw how he recreated this hurt through interactions with his wife. Gradually, he put away his critical demeanor and learned to respond more appropriately to others.

This critical, demeaning approach to others does not get them to respond favorably to you. It does not motivate them to change or reform. It simply causes them to reject or hate you, which may be what you are unconsciously provoking. It's true that emotional terrorism makes some people give you what you want. But at what price? Such outbursts may protect your own flagging sense of self but ultimately make you look bad. If you are prone to angry demeaning outbursts, ask yourself, "What is the purpose of this outburst? What do I hope to gain from this tirade?"

Passively being silent to such abuse does not change or reform the abuser. Taking the beating only "enables" the other person to continue his mistreatment. Angry outbursts or silent suffering are both indications of an underlying attachment to criticism and disapproval.

Lisa, a young college student, told me about an incident with her boyfriend that left her feeling angry and rejected.

One evening after dinner he noticed some books she was

reading on the coffee table. "You're reading these!" he exclaimed. "I can't stand detective novels, they're so poorly written."

Lisa instantly felt crushed and criticized. She froze up inside and told her boyfriend to leave. For the rest of the evening she sulked and stewed over this "put down," taking it as an assault on her worthiness.

I asked Lisa where her sensitivity to criticism might have originated. She replied, "I had an older sister who throughout most of my life told me how stupid and ugly I was and how I had poor taste. She repeatedly told me that no one could like me because I was so dull and unattractive. I believed every word and felt unwanted and undesirable. She always tried to make me look bad."

"Now we can see," I responded, "what happened with your boyfriend. In that moment, he 'became' a psychological copy of your sister by telling you that you have poor taste in books, which in your mind means that you're inadequate. You automatically searched his comment for a hint of unworthiness, and you felt undesirable and rejected as you had so often with your sister."

We all want to blame others for our low opinion of ourselves. But other peoples' words have no power in themselves; it is your reaction to them that becomes the problem. We let words harm us only to the degree that we resonate emotionally with their critical allegations. Children tend to confuse reality with words. Later, as adults, we latch onto what others say about us and respond emotionally as if it were true. We perpetuate the feeling of being undesirable and expect others to see us that way.

The more you anticipate being looked down upon or disapproved of, the more sensitive you are to other people's feedback, and the more distance you create between yourself and others. The more distance you create, the more license you have to feel they do not approve of you.

If you plan your life to avoid possible rejection and disapproval, you lock yourself into feeling unimportant and devalued. You make yourself even more dependent on their reactions, and consequently you lose your sense of who you are. You live in fear.

One way you try to avoid rejection and disapproval is to manage the impressions others have of you by performing in ways that you think people expect of you. In essence, you allow yourself to be controlled by what others want or by their perceptions of you. As a result, you live your life according to someone else's terms rather than being yourself and seeking your own aspirations. By making yourself dependent on someone else's impressions, you disconnect from yourself. You then tend to withhold from others in order to ward off potential disapproval.

Remember, if you are constantly seeking approval and are dependent on how others see you, you are unconsciously attached to *not getting* approval; you are attached to being disliked, devalued, disrespected, and disapproved of. If you were not "into" being disapproved of, then approval by others would not be a burning desire. Approval would be something you automatically give yourself or feel in yourself.

Take a moment and reflect on your need for approval. How much approval is enough? Even when you do get approval, do you find ways to discount it? What would it take to make you feel good about yourself? How can you be really sure other people like and approve of you? If you really think about these questions, you see there can never be enough approval or validation to feel satisfied. It is like pouring water in a bottomless glass.

A good exercise is to keep a journal of the critical judgments you make of yourself. Also, record any real or imagined negative judgments coming from others. Notice how much time and energy you spend thinking about yourself and how others see you. Keeping a journal helps you become more observant of your negative expectations and how you pursue disapproval.

A person who is *not* hooked on disapproval does not need to be liked by everyone. Nor does he focus on the one person who puts him down. He does not waste his energy arranging his life to avoid possible rejection. Approval is simply not a primary motivation for his actions and behavior. He acts or performs for the pure pleasure of it, not for the reaction he may receive. He is "into" being himself, rather than striving to create some impossible ideal.

Once an individual sees how much his attachment to disapproval is woven into his emotional life, he can take steps to extricate himself from this strangling web. Automatically, his self-esteem increases.

The Dart Board

Linda, 35, expressed her feelings about approval in this way: "I accept and take in every little put-down, every derogatory remark I hear or think I hear. I take them in like darts and feel wounded. I expect that others will look down on me and see me as no good, stupid, incompetent, or bad. How I see myself is based on how I perceive that others see me, or how I think they're perceiving me. I accept their point of view as correct and disregard my own opinions as wrong. I know logically I'm an adequate person, but if another person doesn't agree with my viewpoints, then my opinions feel wrong and his are automatically right."

She recalled many times accepting the opinions and assessments about herself from family members. Whenever she did speak up, she was told, "Who asked you?" or "You just do what we want you to do. Don't question your parents!" Linda felt she had no right to ask for anything for herself. She assumed that her words and feelings had no value, so she abandoned her own thoughts and ideas and went along with those of others.

Linda grew up with the notion that any form of independent or free thought was forbidden. To be loved, she had to think like her parents. She had felt stifled and shut down and, no matter how well she performed, expected criticism and disapproval. Later, she provoked criticism by becoming excessively emotional and rebellious, thereby making the negative judgments of others appear to be valid. Over time, Linda let go of her willingness to be a "dart board" for others and developed more confidence and inner serenity.

In many cases, our feelings of disapproval are exaggerated emotional reactions that do not correspond with the facts. Justin, a lawyer, had a strong reaction to the success of a competitor. He took this person's success as evidence of his own inadequacy, feeling it indicated he was inferior. His feeling was totally inappropriate. Justin was successful and well regarded. But on an emotional level he held onto the feeling of being disapproved of and disqualified.

Another caterer remarked, "Every time I assert my opinions of what I want, I feel I have to justify it or give reasons why I feel the way I do. If I say to someone that I want to buy a black dress, I feel compelled to tell them why: 'It's on sale, black is in right now, I need it to match a blouse I bought,' and so on. I expect others will oppose my wants and independent actions or disapprove of them. I defend myself before they give their disapproval. I also expect they will misunderstand my motives and judge me in a negative way."

Members of the Emotional Catering Service either line up before a firing squad prepared to be shot down with verbal bullets, or they feel they are under a microscope—

constantly being inspected, assessed, appraised, and evaluated.

Fear of Exposing Yourself

It took Cassie, a secretary, months of therapy before she would reveal her artwork to me. As I appraised her art, Cassie shielded her face with her hand and looked down with embarrassment. Cassie had talent but did not think of herself that way.

"Why didn't you do something with your talent," I asked her.

Cassie blushed and replied, "Oh, I'd be terrified to show anyone my art. I'm sure they would see it as ordinary. Besides, I'm not too comfortable receiving attention from anyone, even positive attention. I don't like drawing attention to myself. Just thinking about it now makes my heart race."

Cassie avoided parties or social gatherings. In social encounters, she glanced away or looked down to avoid eye contact. It was as though she was saying, "Please don't look at me and I won't look at you. Pretend I am not here."

Cassie's father was a blue-collar worker who used to come home tired and exhausted and drink himself into a stupor in front of the TV. He rarely communicated with his wife or children. Cassie felt invisible to her father who never talked directly to her or asked her questions about herself. She drew pictures as a child but kept her drawings to herself. Only hard physical labor impressed her father. Consequently, she never showed her art to her parents because, as she put it, "They really did not care about me or my talents."

Cassie's father had ignored her, and now Cassie ignored others. She also overlooked and ignored herself, doing to herself what her father had done to her. She became oblivious to her own feelings and needs. To deal

153

with the hurt of being so neglected, Cassie anticipated that others would not take an interest in her. By not exposing her talent, however, Cassie made sure others overlooked her. Her reluctance to reveal her creativity promoted the pain she tried to escape.

Cassie was the one to decide how much good to receive from the world around her. With her mind set on being ignored, no amount of "positive feedback" could penetrate her attachment to being ignored. As long as Cassie needed to feel ignored, she failed to internalize acknowledgment or love from others.

Don't Think Too Much of Yourself

Every time Clarissa had bragged or felt good about a project she finished at school, her mother said, "Don't let this go to your head now. Don't think too much of yourself. Don't get your hopes up." Clarissa grew up associating success with being egotistical and selfish, and as a result she had sabotaged herself and failed to attain her career aspirations. Whenever she did perform well, she apologized for herself and played down her accomplishment. She believed her attainments would provoke a negative reaction from others, just as they had with her mother.

Clarissa secretly had fantasies of fame and fortune. She felt shame when she finally revealed to me her wish to be well- known and successful. Unconsciously, Clarissa was attached to the belief that her voice, her points-of-view, did not matter and that others regarded her as nobody special. She had taken her mother's comments to heart and acted them out in her life.

When caterers like Clarissa feel good about themselves and their accomplishments, they tend, in their own mind, to model their parents and block the good feelings with phrases such as, "Who do you think you are? You're nothing. You'll never amount to anything. What makes you think you're so smart? Don't get such a big head and think too much of yourself."

Some people become perfectionists. In doing so, they attempt unconsciously to solve their attachment to disapproval and criticism. They try to ward off the prospect of being criticized by being perfectionistic. If you are perfect, then no one can judge you as unfit and defective. The need to be perfect, like the need to be approved of, is a defense against the inner attachment to feelings of being less, unworthy, inadequate, and condemned.

Since the state of perfection is subjective (everyone has their own definition of what perfect means) and unattainable, the compulsive pursuit of perfection offers the perfect whip to abuse yourself. The struggle for perfection is fraught with self-punishment, worry, tension, fear, and self-reproach.

The perfectionist feels chronically dissatisfied, disappointed, and let down by her own behavior and that of others. She is known to set unrealistic goals, only to fall short and feel dissatisfied. If she makes a mistake, she considers herself a failure. By beating herself up for allegedly not performing well enough, she reinforces inner feelings of being defective. She imposes on herself the same rejection and disapproval she believed her parents imparted to her. The rigid, critical model of parenting that resides within herself perpetuates the negative judgment she perceived getting as a child.

Rather than a drive to master new challenges, perfectionism represents the pursuit of self-depreciation. Such self-depreciation occurs not only at times of failure, but is an ongoing emotional experience that undermines self-satisfaction even when things are going well. Despite their achievements, perfectionists rarely exhibit any confidence or self-satisfaction. Even when they do get, they are unable to digest their achievement, and they remain emotionally "empty." Compulsive perfectionism represents the unconscious attachment to the struggle to get nowhere, all the while creating the impression of trying so hard to get somewhere. Perfectionists put in lots of time and effort but never get the prize.

The outstanding career success of some perfectionists masks the inner devastation of continuous self-reproach. This may be partly what accounts for the so-called "empty lives" of many successful people. In spite of their success, they still feel empty or not good enough. Perfectionism is an empty state because it represents the illusion of omnipotence in the image of the perfect self. This image masks the inner reality of an imperfect self and all the feelings that go with being imperfect, mainly shame and guilt.

To have no flaws or problems is an unrealistic expectation. Striving to be perfect or to become some idealized fantasy of efficiency creates a split within the self. You put up a false façade that puts you at odds with yourself.

Where does perfectionism come from? When a child needs confirmation of his parents' love and approval, he believes that if he performs to meet their expectations, he will be loved and accepted. Many children grow up feeling belittled or shamed for not being able to satisfy parental expectations. As adults, they continue the belittling process, and sometimes even exaggerate it, by regarding themselves and their efforts as inadequate. Unconsciously they recycle the feeling of being looked down upon as "bad" and not liked.

The child, and later the adult, learns to feel unconsciously secure in the feeling of being shamed, disapproved of, and put down. To mask this secret attachment, he strives to excel. "No, it's not true I look to be judged harshly by others and criticized. Look how much energy I put into doing a perfect job. I really want to be praised and admired." But even when he does excel, this person cannot feel the satisfaction of accomplishment. He does not see or appreciate his successes. He focuses instead on what he did not do or what he could not achieve. He focuses on the "wrong" in what he does.

The perfectionist does something else that is peculiar. He subjects other people to the critical treatment that he gives himself or expects to get from others. He becomes the critical parent to others, judging them harshly, reveling in their mistakes, and seeking out their flaws. He cannot accept or feel satisfied with the behavior and actions of those around him, inwardly feeding on feelings of being let down and disappointed. He also indirectly experiences through the other's shame and debasement the shame and debasement he himself experienced as a child.

The extent to which individuals are critical and judgmental of others is a reflection of how they themselves are unconsciously attached to being judged and criticized, first in a self-critical sense and then in terms of feeling criticized by others. When an individual understands and resolves his inner attachment to disapproval, he automatically becomes more accepting of others.

The perfectionist finds it difficult to embrace his humanity. He focuses on the impression his accomplishments will create, rather than on the "pleasure" he might get from the pursuit of excellence. He cannot enjoy his life because he cannot be human—he must be superhuman. And if he is not superhuman, then he is caught in the emotional conviction of being nothing.

Learn to Accept Yourself
- Recognize daily how non-accepting and judgmental you are of yourself. Write down ways

you goad or berate yourself. Realize that you alone maintain this system of self-reproach and self-negation.

- Where do these negative judgments come from in your past? What did your parents believe about you and your abilities? Locate old childhood perceptions and beliefs that you continue to hold onto today. Realize that you continue the hurt you received in childhood by hurting yourself now.
- Learn to accept and work with criticism from others. Listen to what others say about you. Watch your tendency to become defensive. Watch how much time and energy you invest in worrying about how others see you. Let others see you without being self-centered about it.
- Learn to define your feelings and understand why things bother you. Speak up when something upsets you.
- Think of how many of your thoughts and feelings have to do with past injustices, grievances, and slights. Compare your negative thinking with the time you spend thinking positive thoughts about yourself and life. See if you can go through one day without thinking negative thoughts about yourself or others.
- Watch whether your decisions or actions are based on what you really want or need or based on the acknowledgment and approval of others.
- List all the times you held yourself back or sabotaged success for fear of disapproval or negative evaluation. Ask yourself: "If I fail to go for success or fail to express my dreams and aspirations, what do I get to feel?
- Imagine yourself being successful. Are there any negatives to this picture? For example, one client felt that success would result in other people

clinging to her and wanting her to take care of them. Another client felt that success would rob him of free time.

- Thoughts to consider: a) The world is not absorbed and focused on your performance or how good you are; b) It is okay not to be liked by everyone; c) You do not have to believe what others tell you about yourself; d) Being yourself, without pretense or apology, does not mean that others reject you or abandon you.

Exercises

Write out a description of yourself, your personal qualities, skills, talents, and abilities. How do you feel about yourself? How do you feel you should be better? Why should you be better?

Write out how you imagine others see you. Connect these feelings and expectations with how you felt your parents or siblings saw or reacted to you.

Keep a journal and write down examples of when you feel (real or imagined) criticized, disapproved of, or rejected in your present life. See how many examples you can collect. Notice how hard it is to let go of these feelings.

Answer the following questions:

- What is the worst thing that would happen if I do not finish the tasks on my list perfectly?
- Why is it so hard to be good to myself?
- How does it feel to imagine others admiring, loving, and accepting me?
- What is it like to believe that the world is a loving place that is concerned with my best interests?

Chapter 10
Fear of Intimacy

ECS Creed:
- When your partner gets close or affectionate, harp on his flaws or make an issue of something he did not do right. Pursue intimacy at inappropriate times, such as when your partner is sick or exhausted, or simply ignore your partner's intimate advances and pretend they did not happen.
- Act extremely needy and make frequent requests for assurance that you are loved. Become demanding and insist that your partner give to you right now.
- Accuse your partner of having an intimacy problem and analyze where this problem comes from.
- When your partner brings up personal emotional material, pretend you do not hear, or retaliate verbally, or, better yet, get up and leave.

We are all familiar with the story of the princess who kisses the frog and watches him turn into a prince. But many of us experience the reverse, we kiss a prince and later watch him turn into a frog!

Early in relationships, we experience an initial excitement that our deepest needs for love and emotional security are at last going to be met. But emotional caterers have a variety of methods to turn the promise of love and fulfillment into sour disappointment.

A caterer is dependent on the lover to feel good about herself and to absolve herself of inner guilt and doubt. Consequently, her happiness is extended on credit and eventually the frog appears. When that happens, the caterer pursues the relationship like a drug addict who needs more drug to get the same high.

Now the improvement game begins. The purpose is to make your partner a better individual so he can fulfill your emotional needs and compensate for the lack of emotional nourishment you experienced in childhood. The game is played by subtly controlling and manipulating your partner to behave the way you want.

As a caterer, however, you distance yourself from intimacy because it is threatening and unfamiliar. You feel safer in the role of fixer, reformer, or giver. "When I was in the caretaking role with my first husband," a caterer noted, "I felt confident and in control. My second husband was strong and did not need fixing. For some reason, I lost my confidence with him and became passive and insecure."

Attempts to control your partner mask an inner attachment to being controlled or dependent on someone who lets you down and disappoints you. Intimacy does not flourish under such conditions.

The unconscious dynamics involved in relationships can create misery. Common sense tells us that people who felt unloved and deprived as children will search out and find relationships that finally give them the love, nourishment, and validation they missed. But this is not how it works for most people. They are under an unconscious compulsion to relive the painful emotional issues they experienced with their parents.

We become emotionally attached to people with whom we can recreate the same emotional experiences of our childhood. Once the relationship is secure, latent emotional issues from our past become activated. Our partner awakens memories of childhood pain, which is why many people avoid commitment altogether. We are compelled to repeat or relive the distressing emotional

161

experiences we had with our parents and siblings.

Many of us unconsciously try to reverse the pain and powerlessness we experienced with our parents and siblings by acting like our parents or siblings. We subject our partners to the same emotional treatment we passively experienced as children. If we felt shamed or criticized by a dominating parent, we turn, in our worst moments, into a caricature of that parent and treat our partners in the critical manner that we endured. We respond like a child who, having received a scolding from her mother, turns around and punishes her little brother in a similar manner.

Our partners are mirrors of ourselves. We rarely respond to our partners as they are, but as we "see" them according to our own hidden emotional issues. For example, a man criticizing his wife for laziness or indifference may be masking his own resistance to being more vital and alive. A woman accuses her husband of infidelity because she herself has fantasies of being unfaithful. What we hate the most in our partners is often what we do not want to see in ourselves.

The major barrier to intimacy is the unconscious expectation of loss, helplessness, abandonment, betrayal, rejection, domination, and deprivation. Regardless of our positive gains or accomplishments, we are tempted to dwell on lost love, unattainable love, fantasy love, or a future love. We are compulsively attracted to people who are withholding emotionally and who will not be good for us or who are unwilling to commit to us.

We find ourselves pursuing someone we cannot have or pushing away someone who is there for us. There is an attraction to difficult relationships that mirrors our stormy childhood relationships with our parents. We are out of touch with our real sexual and emotional feelings because of childhood yearnings for approval and affirmation.

"If I put my trust in someone, I expect that he will

eventually reject me," one caterer lamented. "I'll do something to turn him off, and he'll see that I'm ugly and shun me. I know no one can love the real me." Many of us are convinced we have a "fatal flaw" that makes us undesirable. Harboring fatal flaws gives us a feeling of power that we cause the rejection or abandonment we anticipate.

Often when it feels that a relationship is getting too close, we tend to drive away our partner by provoking a fight or stewing over a flaw, thereby creating a "safe" distance. Once separation or abandonment is felt, we try to pull our partner back into the relationship. Why is it that we push away someone who is available, or pursue the one who is hard to get? Why do we reject others before they reject us?

A clue was provided by a man with a history of failed relationships. "All I want is to be close and loved by another human being," he insisted. In each relationship, however, he found all kinds of serious flaws in his partners. By reducing his partner, he justified his avoidance of love and closeness. "It's not that I shy away and avoid intimacy," he protested, "it's just that the other person is so weak. How can I possibly get something from someone who's so flawed and weak?" But this man found intimacy threatening because it brought up in him feelings of potential abandonment, betrayal, and domination, which were feelings he had experienced with his mother. Love was associated with unresolved negative emotions.

We often avoid people who are giving and caring, finding them boring or unattractive. Instead, we become aroused by those who are not able to give emotionally or be there for us. We set ourselves up to replay the emotional hurt of being up against parent figures who were not there for us and who we felt did not value us. Our complaints against our partners are similar to the complaints we had against our parents. We are addicted

163

to recycling old familiar feelings of disappointment and lack of support. Rather than finding caring partners who compensate for our "deprived" childhoods, we unconsciously draw ourselves into emotional dramas that enable us to relive past feelings of abandonment and rejection.

Cindy, a journalist, showed this pattern in her relationships. "When my boyfriend wasn't available to me or when I thought he was interested in someone else, I pursued him and wanted him desperately," she said. "When he asked me to marry him, I lost interest and pulled away, even though he treated me well. I try to find things wrong to justify not staying with him. Every time we have a disagreement, I feel that he's not the right person and I get a strong urge to leave him. When I was growing up, if guys showed interest in me, I felt there had to be something wrong with them. They were weak in my eyes. I would talk myself out of them. The better a guy treats me and the more he loves me, the more I lose respect for him and the less he turns me on."

Cindy could not handle being loved for herself. As much as she claimed she wanted love, she either pushed it away or discounted it when it become available. Being loved frightened her because it brought up childhood feelings of being abandoned and mistreated. Cindy's past was marred by a self-absorbed alcoholic mother and a father who rarely was home. Since she seldom felt close to her parents or siblings, she was not accustomed to feeling loved.

As children, many caterers felt emotionally ignored and neglected. They felt unimportant as their parents pursued their own personal agendas. Caterers transfer onto their partners this old expectation of being abandoned or devalued. Even when their partners do act in a caring manner, caterers look for evidence that it is still not enough.

When one of my clients went off to play bridge with her friends, her husband sulked and felt abandoned. When she wanted to walk alone, her husband accused her of rejecting him. Even when she read a book, she saw a sullen reaction on his face. Her husband unconsciously looked for opportunities to feel abandoned and rejected.

When Intimacy Means Submission and Rejection

I asked several emotional caterers to reflect on this question: "How would you react if someone came along who professed to love you for yourself and wanted to commit to a permanent, loving relationship?"

Their responses revealed fears of rejection, helplessness, and feeling controlled. "I wouldn't have my own life anymore," one woman remarked. "I feel I'd have to give up my life, my privacy, my freedom to take care of his needs. I don't expect to get anything of value from a man, just a feeling of being trapped. I'd have to take care of him and owe him everything. He'd just drain me and take everything from me."

Those were the same feelings she experienced as a child with her father. Growing up, this woman perceived that her father's needs were paramount and that her role was to serve him. Her mother also had sacrificed for the father. For both mother and daughter, intimacy was connected with self-sacrifice, submissiveness, and loss of emotional identity.

Many caterers give up their identities in a relationship. They associate love and closeness with submission and subservience. It is no wonder they shy away from closeness, even when they are in a committed relationship.

A male caterer remarked, "I'll feel sentenced and trapped for the rest of my life. The other person will get into my space, butt in on my life, and become critical and controlling. I'll have to do things I won't like and give into

165

her way of doing things." This man imagined he would be controlled and dominated by a woman, which is how he felt his mother had treated him. He saw relationships as an unavoidable repetition of old feelings of being forced to do what a woman wanted.

We define intimacy according to the manner in which our parents interacted with each other. If we witnessed our parents fighting a lot, then we learned to associate intimacy with conflict. If our parents rarely communicated with each other, or rarely argued, then we associated intimacy with withholding ourselves.

Many children are not encouraged to speak their minds, assert their opinions, or reveal true feelings. As adults, we have difficulty opening up and sharing feelings. Giving in to our feelings feels unfamiliar and vulnerable. We are compelled to respond emotionally according to what we learned as children. But if a person cannot express his feelings or feels intimidated by his partner, he cannot be intimate.

Some of us cut out of our lives those who are causing us problems, rather than trying to understand why we react the way we do or work through our issues. Or we try to avoid threatening situations in our relationships. Some think that emotional independence means not needing relationships. This attitude, along with the need for "space," indicates an attempt to avoid taking responsibility for our own reactions and evading fears of rejection or control.

A young businessman feared commitment because he was sure he would marry the wrong person and miss out on the perfect woman. This man experienced women like a gambler studying racehorses. He expected to be deprived and starved, as he had experienced his relationship with his mother. An emotional addiction to disappointment and missing out accounted for his resistance to commitment.

The root cause of most marital distress is our lingering self-centered childhood perspective. We view our partners through the "eyes" of the starved and rejected child on the lookout for evidence that we are being refused, criticized, dominated, or unloved.

Because of this child-centered perspective, caterers cannot comprehend the concept of mutual cooperation in a relationship. Equal participation, with no one person in a more dominant position, is a foreign concept. Being in a relationship to them means carrying the burden of the other person's needs and expectations. They care for their partners as they wished to be taken care of as children. The drive to take care of the other masks the caterer's emotional need to be taken care of. What most caterers call intimacy is in fact dependency.

In the beginning, the caterer adjusts himself to the other person. He forgets his own needs and preferences in an attempt to please the other person. Pleasing becomes an insurance policy for love and approval. But when he becomes what he believes the other person wants, he loses contact with himself, his real feelings, and even the other person. He begins to control his partner and his partner's emotional reactions by being "helpful and giving."

Eventually, the caterer feels controlled by his partner's authority and struggles to become free. Anger surfaces as he compares the positive feelings at the beginning of the relationship to the negative feelings he is now experiencing. If he fails to get his partner to change, he becomes bitter about the imbalance between what he believes he is giving and the little he feels he is getting in return. He feels used, exploited, and overlooked. He is left in a quandary, feeling available and responsible for his partner but wanting freedom to do as he chooses. The story of Eileen illustrates this pattern.

Eileen's Story

Eileen came to me for psychotherapy after her second marriage seemed about to fail. "When I graduated from high school," she said, "I intended to go to college and become a teacher. A year later, I fell in love with a man I believed to be loving and intelligent. Soon my career goals took a back seat. I remember having some ambivalent feelings about him, but I discounted them because he loved me and wanted me. My friends warned me about his character, but I ignored them and played down his irrational behaviors.

"A year after I married him, I found out this wonderful guy was a dictator. He ordered me around and always found something to criticize. I let him influence my feelings, values, and even political judgments, and I never disagreed with him. I tried to make things better by trying harder to please. When I spoke out or complained, he convinced me it was my fault, that I was neurotic, and I believed him. I worried incessantly whether he would reject me or abandon me. I didn't want to hurt his feelings. My feelings, of course, didn't matter.

"My career aspirations faded, supplanted by daily concerns such as keeping the refrigerator stocked with his favorite foods and keeping the bathtub cleaned of the ring he abhorred. I made sure dinner was ready exactly when he arrived home. In spite of my domestic efforts, he often stayed out late without phoning. I remember one incident when he came home late with alcohol on his breath and became enraged that supper was cold and not to his liking. I was slammed against the wall. I was terrified. Taking the blame as I always did, I apologized and made excuses for what I'd failed to do.

"He was indifferent, cold, and insensitive, yet I overlooked his transgressions, falling back on excuses for his behavior and talking the blame. Often, I'd think it was my stupidity or incompetence that drove him to mistreat me. I wanted to believe that things would get better at any moment. Or I'd convince myself, 'I've put so much into this relationship, I can't quit now. He really didn't mean it, he had too much to drink.' I focused on the good times and ignored the bad, all the while hoping he'd see what a good loving person I was and love me. I always felt I could handle it. I directed my efforts toward turning him into a better person.

"I was required to have sex with him every night whether I wanted to or not. He had three affairs that he expected me to forgive without any remorse on his part. After every abusive episode, he'd come back to me the next day and apologize. I'd get roses or a nice dinner. He would always promise to do better and seek counseling. But these promises were soon forgotten."

I asked Eileen why she had put up with this behavior.

"To think of ending the relationship sent me into a panic. I was terrified of being abandoned and alone. I believed I couldn't manage my life without someone giving me direction. Besides I thought I could never again find a man to love me. I loved him in spite of all the pain he caused me."

I suggested the issue had not been so much about loving her ex-husband as it was about being entangled in feelings of betrayal, criticism, and abandonment. She associated being loved with being abused. "Who does your first husband remind you of?" I asked her.

"He's just like my father. My dad was an alcoholic who was withholding, unreliable, and extremely critical. He ordered us around like a dictator, insisting that we obey his every command immediately. I had to keep the house sparkling clean. There were several occasions when I was slapped for not washing the dishes well enough. He made me do them over. He was always right and did not tolerate back talk. I was called lazy and incompetent. Dad also stayed out drinking a lot, while Mom waited and cried. I never remember getting an ounce of praise or positive attention. It's amazing. This is what I'm experiencing with my first husband—feeling hurt, rejected, betrayed, devalued, and abandoned.

"But why would I do that? Why did I seek out those same feelings of hurt? It sounds so irrational. It just doesn't make sense to me."

"You have become accustomed to those feelings," I explained. "Without having any other model, you assumed this is how relationships are. You associate love with being mistreated and controlled. Even though you protested this behavior, you really do not expect relationships to be any other way. As a child, you felt mistreated and controlled, and you concluded that this was the way you were supposed to be treated. All of us set ourselves up unconsciously to endure as adults what we endured with our parents. It also appears that you copied your mother's lifestyle. Can you tell me more about your mother?"

"My God, I hate to hear that. I swore I would never be like her," Eileen replied. "I love my mother but I'm angry with her for not standing up to Dad and challenging his behavior. She just took Dad's abuse and pretended nothing was wrong. She never defended me or stood up for me. Because she did nothing to stop Dad, I felt responsible for his behavior. I was sacrificed because Mother couldn't deal with Dad. Since all the attention was focused on him, I felt shut out from closeness with Mom and believed I wasn't important enough to be listened to or taken seriously. You're right, I acted out just like her in my marriage and took my husband's abuse. I didn't realize this before. I guess I just didn't want to see it."

Eileen had not wanted to hurt her ex-husband's feelings, even though she was aware of the abuse. This apparently altruistic attempt to spare his feelings (along with her fear of being on her own and responsible for her life) was a cover-up for her own unconscious attachment to being neglected, rejected, mistreated, and dominated. There is only one reason for staying in an abusive relationship and that is the attachment to being abused. Being abused feels normal and familiar.

After Eileen divorced her first husband, she entered a relationship with a man who was gentle and kind. He let her do more or less what she wanted and was emotionally supportive. Shortly after they married, however, she became restless and sexually unresponsive. She began to have dreams and fantasies of her first husband.

"My second husband was caring but passive," Eileen remarked. "He went along with my decisions and rarely protested. Our communication was barren and consisted of talk about daily schedules. He was not aggressive with his career. I criticized him for the way he dressed, his slowness, and his inability to confront or argue. I focused on what he was doing wrong or what he wasn't doing for me. I became the dominant partner who advised him and directed his life.

"Every time he forgot to run an errand, I was furious. Every time he was late, I felt he did it on purpose to make me suffer. While I took on all the responsibility for the relationship, he was out having fun, getting away with not doing his duties. I felt cheated and deprived of attention and help. There I was again feeling disappointed and abandoned, but only in a different way."

"In this marriage," I told her, "you became like your father and unknowingly subjected your second husband to the same kind of treatment you passively endured from your father and first husband. To avoid being a victim of an oppressive male again, you identified with the aggressor and became the one who dominated. Your fantasies of your first husband indicate that you miss the domination and mistreatment that you experienced in that relationship. Obviously, you found that kind of treatment more exciting than being given to and allowed to do what you wanted."

In both her marriages, Eileen's dreams of intimacy had faded into familiar feelings of rejection and emotional starvation. By working through her negative attachments to these feelings, she finally achieved a satisfying relationship with her second husband.

With uncanny ability, the unconscious inner child draws to us those individuals who will fulfil our expectations of disappointment and rejection. In spite of our conscious efforts to attain love and contentment, we are destined to repeat our old childhood hurts in our relationships.

Eileen's emotional addiction to her first husband is similar to an alcoholic's attachment to his bottle. "I felt as though I had no choice but to stay with him, she said. "I was caught up in something bigger than myself, and I was helpless and powerless to do anything about it. I convinced myself I was in control of the situation, and that I could work it out on my own."

Relationship addicts unconsciously collude with abusive partners through learned childhood passivity and helplessness. They have grown up willing to accept mistreatment, and they mistakenly associate mistreatment with getting attention or being loved. Hooked on degradation and domination, they unknowingly reinforce and encourage mistreatment through their passivity, thus recreating their childhood relationships with abusive parents or siblings.

In accounting for their relationship problems, most people blame their partners or blame themselves for the wrong reasons. Passive partners often exclaim, "I withdraw because you intimidate me." Dominant partners respond, I'm so aggressive because you withdraw and take no action." Both feel: "I am how I am because you are like you are. If you were different, then I would be different too."

Your partner's behaviors often serve as alibis for your own self-defeating behaviors. These are typical alibis, "I haven't attained the success I'm supposed to because my husband discourages me and won't support me." Or, "If only she would get off my case and stop nagging me so much, maybe I wouldn't drink so much."

The Begging Bowl Syndrome

Emotional caterers approach relationships like supplicants carrying a begging bowl. "Feed me, love me, support me, make me feel I'm special," they plead. "Give me all the love and validation I never received growing up. I'm just an unloved orphan."

For these people love implies a demand, a payment. "If I love you, then I expect a positive response in return. If I do not feel you are giving back to me, I feel refused or rejected and I withhold my love." Pseudo-love is bargaining for love, "If you do this for me, then I'll do that for you. I'll take care of you, if you will take care of me."

Your partner is approached not as a real person with needs and desires of his own but as a resource for the satisfaction of your own frustrated needs. You spend energy to get the "desired response" from your partner, rather than opening up and sharing your own feelings or appreciating your partner as he or she is.

Most people enter into a relationship with a fantasy of how it should be and what they should get. This fantasy is created by thoughts, feelings, and perceptions based on their past childhood relationships. Attempts are made to control the relationship to fit their fantasy or ideal. The relationship is measured by the criteria they impose on it. They push their partner toward emotional reformation to get the love and acceptance they cannot give themselves.

As a caterer, you assume to know what is best for your partner, and you make it your job to prop him up.

Your attempts to "repair" your partner mask your unconscious attachment to being dependent on someone who disappoints you and lets you down. You fear you will not get emotional fulfillment if your partner does not change. Unfortunately, that is your unconscious priority— to be emotionally starved.

You believe your loved one has the capacity to neutralize negative feelings, satisfy your needs, and make you feel good about yourself. Your partner is seen as the ultimate provider, liberating you from the emotional or financial responsibility of your life. This fantasy is based on an idealized mother-child relationship.

When you seek fulfillment of your needs through another, you are not loving that person. You are more interested in your pleasure, your experience, your needs, your wants. When you expect the other to be different than the way he is, you are not loving him. If you "love" your partner when he serves you and hate him when he doesn't, you are not loving him. You are involved with yourself, your own needs for control, and your unresolved emotional issues.

Trouble begins when two people meet with their begging bowls outstretched. "You fill mine first and then I'll fill yours." Score is kept on whose bowl gets filled most. "You starve me out, so I'll starve you out, too." The other person is soon seen as the enemy who is against you and your needs. You are stuck on the notion that you can only attain happiness when your begging bowl is filled by others, meaning the security of feeling that you are deeply loved.

Ironically, the more you try to make love happen and "secure" it for yourself, the more it will elude you and the more you will feel that something is missing in yourself.

It is unrealistic to expect our partners to love us in a way we are convinced our parents never did and to compensate for the wounds and hurts of our childhoods.

Even when someone comes along who is able and willing to fill our bowl, we sabotage the experience or feel it is not enough. The begging bowl is bottomless. The way to resolve this problem is to acknowledge our attachment to *not getting* the love we claim we want.

Love for many caterers covers up fear. When you need someone and regard that as love, you fear he or she will leave you or not love you tomorrow. When you fear loss or hurt, you demand security. But now there's never enough security. Love is not something to contain in a box or possess like a gem. When there is fear of being alone, or demands made based on fear of rejection or abandonment, true love is impossible. A relationship based on such conditions produces more loneliness.

The following stories offer further understanding of the addiction to not getting.

Mindy, a small-business owner, was plagued with chronic dissatisfaction in her relationships with men. Her series of one-to-two-year relationships ended badly. A chauvinistic aristocrat discarded her, a paranoid doctor disgusted her, and a bankrupt developer used her money. It was not just bad luck. She was not rushing to men for happiness, although in the initial stages of her relationships she felt excitement and passion. Rather, she used men for another purpose: they were blamed for her unhappiness.

Mindy's mother had lived in self-inflicted misery. Chronically unhappy despite prosperity, her mother had constantly criticized Mindy's father and blamed him for her problems. From her mother's perspective, Mindy's father never gave her enough, never loved her enough, and never attended to her needs with the right attitude. Mindy reacted the same way with men. While she struggled to be happy, she unconsciously expected (and was attached to) rejection as well as emotional and material deprivation. She chose men who failed to give her the love and satisfaction she craved, thus providing further evidence for her "right" to be disappointed with men.

No man could satisfy or fulfill Mindy's begging bowl requirements. Unconsciously borrowing from her mother's brand of chronic dissatisfaction, she found ways to sabotage her relationships and blame men for her unhappiness. With insight into her problem, Mindy began to understand that she really did not expect to get anything of value from a man. As she came to terms with her own attachment to being deprived and rejected, her latest relationship held out more promise for happiness.

Jeanine, an administrative assistant, also had an unconscious attachment to unavailable men. Her pattern, however, was to be persistently involved with married men. She would fall madly in love with a married man and try to win his heart and his name. Things would go well in the beginning, but just when success (winning the man) was in reach, he would abruptly decide to return to his wife. This left Jeanine devastated and locked for months in a prison of emotional pain. At thirty-five, she was still unmarried, recycling this syndrome of rejection and betrayal.

As a child, she had perceived her mother as distant and cold. Her only acknowledgment came from her father who she idolized. Feeling she could not get emotional sustenance from her mother, she turned to her father who became, in her eyes, her only source of love. But dad, too, was unavailable in the sense that he was married to her mother and supported her mother's behavior. Consequently, Jeanine felt rejected, disappointed, and cast aside by him.

She repeatedly acted out this scene in her relationships with men. Intimacy and passion were followed by abandonment and rejection when the man returned to his wife. She took the rejection as an indication of her unworthiness. I asked Jeanine to describe the feelings when the man left her and to trace that feeling back to her relationship with her parents.

"As a little girl, I felt my mother did not love me or want me. She was always distracted or involved in other things.

There was always this longing, this big empty ache. I was sad and depressed a lot. When a man loves me and wants me, I feel good about myself. If he rejects me and goes back to someone else, then I'm nothing. The pain is losing someone, never being able to win their love. My mother's love was unattainable to me. I could never please her or do anything right. She never praised me or gave me any indication that she liked me. I felt so lonely and angry as a little girl. The pain is feeling unloved and unwanted."

Jeanine kept this pain alive by unconsciously recreating the loss and abandonment of her father and the rejection by her mother. Until she saw and understood this pattern, she was incapable of creating a loving, committed relationship. She finally broke out of this pain cycle and opened herself up to an available man who was ready to commit to her.

James, a businessman, had just ended a four-year relationship fraught with passion and pain. "This past week has been filled with emotions," James sadly revealed. "I've made two very important discoveries about myself. First, I recognize this emotional pain. I've felt it throughout my life. I remember feeling it even as a very small child. I connect this pain with loss or the fear of loss. The loss is that of someone very close to me, a nurturer and caretaker. I felt it as a tiny child when my mother, and to a lesser extent my father, criticized me harshly and unfairly and then withdrew their affection from me. I have managed to experience this loss throughout my life in all of my relationships with women. There was always an old refrain playing in the background that said, 'You will never have any friends, no one will ever love you, no woman will ever want to marry you or stay married to you.'

"Second, I now remember that strife prevailed in all my relationships, going back as far as high school. I often fought and split up with girls. In my marriage, there were times when
I wouldn't settle for anything less than a fight and the threat of divorce. I tried to pick fights with my wife, but she simply didn't know how to fight. I'm sure that's part of the reason I broke off the marriage.

"During this last relationship, I found dozens of reasons to be upset with my partner and to fight with her. Invariably, I would abuse her verbally and then withdraw my affection and presence from her. This is exactly the way my mother treated me. Mother became outraged at my behavior and punished me by withdrawing and shutting me out."

James's anger was a reaction and a defense against his unconscious indulgence in feelings of rejection and abandonment. This was why he fought with the women in his life. He reacted with anger to a perceived threat and became verbally and emotionally abusive (actually provoking them to reject him). Afterwards he withdrew from them. When the damage was done and abandonment seemed imminent, the pain of rejection settled in and he tried to win them back.

James looked for the bad in his partners rather than the good. Even when his partners showed little offensive or threatening behavior, he found some excuse to create a crisis.

After a time in therapy, James said, "I'm working on training myself to stop searching for negative reasons why the relationship won't work. I have stopped looking for opportunities for the lady in my life to reject or abandon me. I'm consciously choosing to enjoy the positive signs and positive experiences. If I don't learn this, I'll never have a lasting, loving relationship."

As these cases illustrate, emotional caterers repeat variations of the familiar emotional scenarios they experienced in their childhoods, in spite of opportunities to create loving environments. They have become unconsciously addicted or attached to pseudo-fathers or pseudo-mothers who dominate, reject, or deprive them. Many mask these unconscious attachments by becoming like their parents and subjecting their partners to the same treatments they received as children.

Survivors of broken relationships prefer to believe they are innocent victims of their partners' malice or deception. They want to blame their partners for the problems in the relationships and are reluctant to consider why they become entangled in such unsatisfied situations. They may spend years gathering evidence from friends and books that "proves" their own innocence.

Because we transfer emotional feelings from the past to the present, we fail to see our partners' perspectives. Rather than understanding how our partners experience events, we jump to erroneous assumptions about their behaviors. We are too defensive and too ready to feel criticized and rejected to be sincerely interested in our partner's perceptions or feelings.

You can understand your partner's perspective by asking direct questions such as: "What do you mean by that?" Or, "How do you interpret what's happening?" Or, "Does this feeling have anything to do with me?"

Changing Your Self-Destructive Partner
What does a dissatisfied caterer do when involved with a partner who is blatantly insensitive or self-destructive?

You must first understand why you chose to be involved with a self-absorbed and emotionally unavailable person. You need to define your unconscious emotional

179

attraction to this individual. Ask yourself, "Who does this person remind me of in my past? What feelings is this person triggering in me, and how do those feelings relate to my experience as a child?

Your inclination is to focus on the flaws and weakness of the other person. However, when you understand how you unconsciously play into the hurtful feelings you are experiencing with this person, you gain the strength and awareness to
hold your own power and make necessary changes.

Here is an example of how this works. Carrie, a college- educated housewife with a three-year-old son, was married to an alcoholic who frequently stayed away from home without phoning. They rarely communicated with each other and sex was infrequent. Carrie was feeling abandoned, rejected, unimportant, and burdened. Because her husband was not dependable, she felt responsible for running the household. Meanwhile, she got little appreciation or cooperation from him. She tried for years to get him into counseling or Alcoholics Anonymous and had threatened to divorce him several times. He would then act like a dog with his tail between his legs, pleading forgiveness and promising he would get help. But he reneged on his promises and his old patterns soon reappeared.

Carrie was exhausted and frustrated by his empty promises yet frightened to go it alone and be independent. Terrified by the prospect of abandonment, she endured his behavior, even though she overtly protested and complained. Her salvation was to begin to look seriously at her involvement with a man who wasn't there for her.

I asked her to write out a relationship history and a description of her experience with both parents. She was asked to compare her relationships with men to her relationship with her father. She also compared her behavior and reaction to her husband with the manner in which her mother had responded to her father.

Carrie had earlier relationships with three men who were emotionally immature and insecure. Two had drug and alcohol problems. She was clearly choosing men who did not display the emotional capacity to be generous and loving.

She was recreating with her husband the same feelings of emotional deprivation and rejection she had endured with her alcoholic father. Her father had provided well for the family but had been emotionally unavailable and excessively demanding. He was away a lot and avoided being involved in the family. When he was home, he was the center of attention, but usually aroused fear and dislike.

Carrie's mother, for the most part, was passive and accepting of her husband's behavior. She claimed she could not leave him because he needed her too much. But she had little self-esteem and feared being on her own.

Carrie could see she was replaying her parent's relationship. She mirrored her mother's passivity and was settling for emotional abandonment. Like her mother, she was centering her life around her husband's needs. With this understanding, she could now begin to work out her dependency, passivity, and self-neglect.

The process of healing involved grieving over the pain of rejection and abandonment by her father. She saw how she was unconsciously attached to being treated in a neglectful manner and how hard it was for her to put her needs and feelings first. Carrie also worked through her absorption of her mother's passivity and self-denial and her own willingness to accept crumbs in her emotional relationships with others.

"But why am I the one who has to get better?" Carrie protested. "Why doesn't he have to come to therapy and work on his problems?"

181

I replied, "You see therapy for yourself as a situation of 'he wins, I lose.' This reflects the power conflict that characterized your relationship. You feel he's getting away with his crimes, as you felt your father was not held accountable. But he's not getting away with anything. The fact that you are working on yourself indicates greater resourcefulness and strength on your part. Your transformation will be your gain, as well as a gain for your child. Think of yourself as an agent for positive change."

Carrie came to understand that her husband's negative behavior was not designed to torture or deprive her. Her husband was trapped in his own emotional predicament, one he did not understand. She learned not to play off his weaknesses to feel rejected and deprived.

When she healed her wounds and grew strong enough to command respect and love, she confronted her husband with power and a new sense of resolve: "Either you get into recovery or the relationship is over." She did not confront him with anger or righteous lectures and protests. Instead, she expressed directly how his behavior hurt her and their child. Calmly, she told him how his alcoholism affected her and how she respected herself too much to continue enduring it.

Carrie's husband felt the change in her and knew she was serious. He chose recovery and abstinence. Both he and Carrie entered marriage counseling. However, after a few months of positive changes in her husband, Carrie developed a strong impulse to leave the marriage. All of her pent-up anger came out in a strong urge to retaliate against him for "all the pain he put me through."

She was also frightened of her husband's positive changes, feeling he would not depend on her or need her any more. She feared the loss of control in the relationship and recognized that her need to control her husband gave her security. Her husband feared that in getting healthy, he would not get any more attention or be taken care of. Both of them feared abandonment and rejection if the relationship changed. They realized how they colluded to serve and satisfy each other's infantile fears and attachments. Within two years, she and her husband were relating in a whole new way.

It had taken Carrie's inner transformation to inspire her husband to face his addiction. In many cases, however, self-destructive partners choose to stay with their addictions. If your partner insists on driving straight for the cliff, you can make the choice to get out of the car and create a new life.

When you stop trying to get your partner to change, your partner often softens and responds more appropriately. Your partner now has the opportunity to see his own behavior, rather than to protest or defend against your demands. When you wean yourself from your attachment to feeling like a victim to his weaknesses, compassion and love can deepen.

True intimacy involves being a friend to your partner and wanting the best for him or her. It means sharing your innermost feelings and needs without fear. Love is the ability to respond emotionally to what is happening with your partner. Both partners, through mutual cooperation and "response-ability," create an atmosphere of openness, affection, and fun. Intimacy implies a joint venture—both partners working on the same team for their mutual happiness.

The best way to resolve your issues with intimacy and closeness is to "get to know yourself." You must see clearly who you are before you can see the other as he or she is. As long as you are trying to get your partner to fulfill some inner need or pre-existing deficiency in yourself, you will not be able to understand or relate to the other person. If you cannot live with yourself, you automatically put demands on others that block the possibility of lasting closeness.

183

When you gain insight into the nature of your unconscious childhood conditioning, you are free to relate to the other person without being overwhelmed or manipulated. No longer depending on your partner for emotional validation, you allow your partner just to be himself or herself. Isn't that something we all want, to be allowed to be who we are, to be loved with all our weakness, and to make our own changes in our own time?

Real love expresses itself when each is free to be who he or she is. Love incorporates concern and caring, but does not seek anything for itself. This concern and caring is not the same thing as needing the other to change. Real love is self-generated and without fear. It frees the people it touches instead of binding them with strings of guilt or expectation.

Exercises
- Ask yourself, "What does the word commitment or marriage mean to me?" Or, "How would I feel if someone came along who truly loved me and wanted to be with me on a permanent basis?"
- Write out your fantasy of the ideal relationship. Ask yourself what it is you are looking for in your fantasy? Notice how you think your partner should be. Why do you want your partner to be this way?
- Note all the expectations you have for your relationship and for your partner. The point is to stand back and see how these expectations affect your relationship and how demands destroy intimacy. Ask yourself, "Can I accept my partner as he is? If not, what is in the way of my acceptance?"
- Write down your relationship history (those persons with whom you have had a significant relationship) and notice recurring themes or patterns in your behaviors and these partners'

responses to you. Compare these relationships to the one you had with your parents. How are they similar?

- In what ways does your partner resemble either your mother or father? Do you feel the same feelings you experienced with your mother and father? Define your feelings.
- Write down ways you sabotage intimacy with your partner. Note how you may provoke your partner into an encounter with the feelings you are having. How does this pattern remind you of your past?

Chapter 11
Childhood Development of the Emotional Caterer

Is our fate predetermined, a result of genes and environmental forces outside of our control? Or do we have choices and options to direct and create our lives?

In the old European model, one's fate was considered to be a condition of blood, ancestry, and status at birth. Personality and character were thought to be determined through genetics and bloodlines. In this old model, willpower and hard work were not considered enough to overcome the limitations of birth into the lower classes.

The American Revolution was partly an attempt to break away from this deterministic mode that settlers in the new world found too limiting. To young America, striving to gain acknowledgment and independence, people had free will and the option to become whatever they wanted. We developed an individualistic society where value is set on talent and accomplishment rather than one's status at birth or one's family name. A clever, motivated person has fewer limits on what he can accomplish or how far he can go. Ideally, each is responsible for his or her own destiny.

But strains of the old deterministic thinking are coming back in a new guise. Addictive behavior, codependency, and depression are being blamed on genes, biochemistry, or a "disease." When we accept the disease model as the explanation for these emotional disorders, once again our fate is determined by something beyond our control. Having "a disease" is easier to accept (than acknowledging our own complicity in our suffering) because it absolves us of responsibility for our plight.

It is also fashionable to blame our mental and

emotional distress on our upbringing—the result of "toxic" parents. We blame not only parents, but spouses, bosses, children, the patriarchy, poverty, and a host of other alleged ills for our personal limitations or failures. Genetic endowments, society, and other external variants are certainly influential. But another determining factor, one which we can learn to moderate to our advantage, concerns each person's unique attitudes and perceptions about himself and the world, as well as the reactions he has and choices he makes as a result of these perceptions.

Let us illustrate with this example. Imagine a hiking trail up a mountain. It is strenuous, filled with obstacles, and at times dangerous. Two people, Dean and Larry, equivalent in physical strength, take on the trail. Dean never makes it to the top, and he returns complaining, "How could I be expected to climb such a difficult trail!"

In contrast, Larry succeeds and reaches the top, feeling joyful in the process. What causes his different response to the mountain? Obviously, it is some quality in Larry that enables him to succeed. He was not defeated by difficult, external conditions.

By making genes or external causes responsible for failures and limitations, an individual may remain stuck in a victim position, emotionally dependent on some outside source to help him manage and accept his fate. This mentality lends itself to depression, powerlessness, and bitterness. The individual believes there is no hope for improvement or gain. He believes that he is stuck with a bad gene, dysfunctional parents, or a bad-luck disease. Consequently, he must wait for society to change or someone else to fix the problem.

Such a position will resolve inner tension to a degree because there is no challenge to prove oneself. The individual has a built-in justification for failure: "I was born with this disease, so I can't help being the way I am.

187

It was in the cards." This mentality frees the individual from personal responsibility and holds others or circumstances responsible for his failures.

Free will and free choice come at a cost. They have the effect of placing us under emotional stress. When we are in a position to become smarter, richer, and more powerful, the inner conscience is going to be saying every time we hesitate or falter, "You're a loser! You were never meant to succeed, and you know it."

Too many choices bring tension and hesitation: "What if I make the wrong choice? I could mess up my life." But the expression of autonomy or individual responsibility (making the most of what you have got) is the only way to inner freedom and the possibility of happiness.

The Belief in Childhood Innocence

Mental-health professionals who believe emotional problems are due solely to faulty parenting assume that the child is a sweet innocent who can be molded like a slab of clay into the likeness and image of his or her parents. These professionals, along with other adults, believe that the child's brain is simply a miniature adult's that needs to be filled with the adult's version of reality. Such people base their theories of infancy and childhood development on subjective and sentimental projections of their own childhood longings, rather than explore or understand the objective research on infant and child perceptions and behaviors.

This belief in childhood innocence becomes a convenient rationalization for present-day misery: "I am not responsible for how my life turned out. I am an innocent victim of my parents' bungling, and if it weren't for them and what they did to me, I would be happy and successful."

Jean Piaget, a renowned expert on child development, believed we are influenced by an interaction of heredity and environment (nature and nurturing). He espoused a concept of evolving consciousness, based on an individual's constant interplay with his environment.

Piaget observed that a child has perceptions that are very different from an adult's. And what the child understands of reality is never a simple copy of his sensory impressions. Reality is interpreted according to the child's own unique way of knowing. Reality is a reconstruction of the environment, never a perfect copy of it.

Another expert on childhood development, psychoanalyst Edmund Bergler, had this to say of the myth that small children are naturally happy and of pure intent: "It is a glorification in retrospect, created by dissatisfied people who, having repressed their own past, nostalgically pursue lost years, hopes not materialized, shattered illusions, now projected in their original shape on their children. The nursery, where the alleged happiness is supposed to blossom, is the place that holds the world record for mutual misunderstandings. Adults misconstrue their children's feelings and children those of adults."

There is a widespread assumption that kind, loving, and understanding parents will produce normal, well-behaved children. If parents learned the correct procedures, this theory contends, the needs of the child would be satisfied and the child would become whole and happy.

But it is not realistic to expect that all parents can be analyzed and cleared of their unresolved childhood issues. Trying to be the perfect parent or paying lip-service to the correct way of responding to your child results in phoniness. Children are affected more by their parents' non-verbal communication and can see through superficial attempts to be perfect parents. The essential understanding is this: There is often little a parent can do to prevent his or her child from seeing injustice in the parent's behavior. What, for instance, are parents to do about a child who repeats the same provocations over and over again, unfazed by their punishments? What about the problem that arises when parents, in being giving and generous, find that their children become insatiable?

Children cannot be spared all disappointment. Experiencing some disappointment is necessary for their adjustments to reality. No matter how well parents succeed in doing right, children still may choose to react or respond negatively to them and their actions. Some parents live in fear of making mistakes that might lead to emotional damage in their children. People who want to blame their emotional or social difficulties solely on their parents' negligence or cruelty are missing the point. A child of such negligent parents still has, in the context of his adult life, to contend with his own unconscious tendencies to continue to feel a victim of injustices in his present life.

It is true that the parents' feelings, beliefs, and behaviors toward the child leave an imprint on his or her psyche. But the child experiences the environment as he sees it and feels it. The child elaborates emotionally on his experience.

Each child's response to how her parents treat her is unique. I have worked with siblings from the same family who shared substantially different views of their parents and what happened to them as children. Parents are unable to control how their children may unconsciously elaborate on what they perceive in their environment. What a child does with what she perceives depends entirely on her own conscious and unconscious choices.

Many adults raised in highly dysfunctional families turn out to be relatively healthy and lead productive lives. Alternatively, children raised in healthy families can still have magnified small injustices, and as adults they continue to interpret situations through painful feelings of disappointment, refusal, loss, criticism, rejection, betrayal, and abandonment. Adults raised by caring parents still can have such unresolved emotional issues. The notion that we would be "happy and satisfied" if only our parents had met all our emotional and physical needs is a fantasy that enables us to avoid taking responsibility for complicity in our emotional problems.

No matter what their home life is like, children see reality through their own inner fantasies, misconceptions, and misinterpretations. The child does not see reality as adults do. For example, if a child is running around the house, making lots of noise, enjoying his play, he is apt to interpret his parents' demands for quiet as, "They don't want me to have fun."

It is true, of course, that a child has genuine needs for love, attention, affection, praise, and support for his or her own autonomy. A child obviously benefits from parents who understand his or her needs and strive to meet them. But total satisfaction of the child's needs is impossible because of the child's natural egocentrism, his self-aggression, and his negative interpretations of his parents' actions and behaviors.

The production of healthy children does not rest solely on the degree to which their emotional needs are met but on how they overcome their infantile conflicts and adopt a relatively objective outlook on reality.

Let me use a personal example. From their early infancies, I noticed a substantial difference in my two sons. One was a high-wired baby who fussed and demanded a lot of attention. When he fed, he acted as though he never got enough, even though he received plenty. He would overeat, spit up, and then eat more. Good caterer that I was, I thought I was doing something wrong, that the problem was with me. If I could just find the magic key, I believed, then he would settle down. I was left with the feeling that I could not satisfy him enough. This child never seemed to get enough food or attention, though I attended to his every need. His pattern of feeling he never got enough persisted into his teenage years, in spite of the nurturing he received.

My other son was completely different. He was easily satisfied and rarely fussed. He was easy-going and handled stressful situations with ease, an ability that persists to this day. I have heard similar stories from other parents who have noticed innate differences in their children. Each child, then, has his own biological endowment which guides the rate and direction of his development, independent of how his parents respond to him.

Effects of Infantile Helplessness and Dependency

In addition to their own unique personality orientations, babies also have traits or components in common. Compared with other animals, humans experience a delayed growth rate. The long prenatal period and extended helplessness in infancy is in sharp contrast to the rest of the animal kingdom, and it appears necessary for the development of the complex human brain and nervous system. This results in a long period of immaturity and helplessness in infancy.

Since human development is slow, infantile traits have more time to become impressed upon the psyche. This drawn-out infantile dependency results in a protracted experience of helplessness, powerlessness, and vulnerability. These feelings persist unconsciously in varying degrees throughout our lives.

Because of this infantile helplessness and dependency, humans retain fantasies of regressing back to the protection of the womb (wanting everything taken care of for us without any effort on our part). Sigmund Freud believed our biological helplessness contributes to the formation of the superego—the inner conscience or inner critic that torments us with guilt, reproach, and shame.

Because an individual has repressed emotions from a past stage of his development, other people in his adult life become duplicate mothers and fathers, and current situations become distorted by lingering childhood perceptions. Our unrealistic beliefs and distressful emotions are based on unconscious childhood fears and perceptions. In other words, we use our present reality to play out unresolved, childhood feelings.

Children, of course, are at the mercy of their caretakers. A baby is completely dependent upon her mother. She is dependent on getting her milk, is passively subjected to a time schedule, and must later undergo the passive experience of weaning. She is helpless as someone forces her to go to bed, and she feels controlled as she is trained in cleanliness.

The feeling of being a helpless victim permeates the life of the infant and persists into adult relationships. The power struggles that characterize adult relationships are recreations of the passive child being controlled by the dominating parent. How we interpreted or experienced our primary relationship with our parents determines how we respond in our adult relationships. Most emotional distress has its origins in the feeling of being a helpless victim or a target of someone else's malice. This feeling of passive victim undermines our creative expression and emotional independence.

The Illusion of Being All-Powerful

According to Jean Piaget and Edmund Bergler, the child enters the world steeped in the illusion of her own omnipotence. This illusion is derived from the protected existence in the womb, where food, oxygen, and safety were provided automatically. An aspect of the infant's struggle after birth is geared toward regaining this paradise, or feeling of omnipotence. Hence, throughout our lives we engage in ongoing struggles for preferential positions or treatment.

At first, the baby ignores the disturbing reality that the womb no longer exists; she does not recognize the outer world. Eventually, when ignoring it or denying it no longer works, the baby cries and protests loudly. As the world makes its presence felt, she begins to feel that its offerings—pleasant and unpleasant—are brought about by her own powers. She moves her hand and Mom puts a rattle in it; in the child's mind, she has given herself the object.

When the child awakes, milk is provided. When she cries, she is picked up. Immediate attendance by mother is misinterpreted as the outcome of her own powers. For the child, the bottle or breast magically appear out of nowhere and enter her mouth. In the child's consciousness, she gives everything to herself out of herself. The child perceives that the mother, and even material objects, are simply extensions of herself. Far from acknowledging her complete dependence on her mother, she believes that she creates for herself, out of herself, everything that she wants and needs. With this perception, gratitude and kindness are taken for granted, and the child expects immediate service and gratification of her wants and needs.

As she grows, the fantasy of being all-powerful comes into conflict with reality. Being controlled in situations such as going to bed, eating, and being dressed, represents to the child an assault on her fantasy of being all-powerful. One painful experience after another shows her the fallacy of her assumption. The baby develops an aversion to being forced to do what the bad outer world (mother) wants her to do. This results in fury and aggression that, because of her limited musculature, she cannot fully express. This fury and aggression is consequently projected onto the parents. Anthropologists have observed that infants from diverse cultures see their parents as ogres, monsters, or witches when the parents break down the child's cherished fantasy of being all-powerful.

Reality, as represented by the actions of the mother, is now refusing her, denying her, and depriving her. Therefore mother (reality) is bad and cruel. Yet she is helpless in the face of her (it). Her little body cannot expel or direct outward all the fury and frustration she experiences, and so the aggression rebounds into her own body where it turns into self-aggression.

Every disappointment the child experiences is an insult to her egocentrism and feeling of being all-powerful. She reacts with frustration and fury, which is projected onto the mother who in reality may be kind and loving. But in the child's fantasy, mother becomes a threatening figure about to devour her or starve her to death. This accounts for the popularity of stories such as "Hansel and Gretel."

Child-development researcher Melanie Klein reported that all children have body-destructive fantasies that are projected onto the mother. These projections are not due to specific social conditions, but to the primitive infantile ego (omnipotence) and its aggressiveness. Klein described several baby fears that may persist throughout our lives. One is fear of being starved, produced by the offense to the child's ego that his mother did not come on demand and by his inability to tolerate any delay when his hunger arises. The baby is insulted when he has to wait even a few minutes for the breast or bottle, and he believes, because he has no sense of future, that since the breast or bottle is not present immediately, it will never come. In the adult, the expectation of being starved is translated emotionally into feelings of being refused love, kindness, gifts, support, and attention, which are emotional substitutes for food.

Another baby fear is of being devoured by the mother. In order to protect himself from this helpless feeling, the baby displays aggressive designs in biting the nipple or bottle. The baby masks its aggressive wishes by projecting those wishes onto its mother. Another fear is of being poisoned by mother. Eventually, the baby has to admit that he is being fed, but he preserves his grievance against his mother by imagining that what she gives is poisonous and harmful. As an adult, the individual will admit he gets from others, but he will often want to believe that what he is getting is inadequate, deficient, or harmful.

Other baby fears include fear of being choked, fear of being chopped to pieces, fear of being drained, and fear of castration. These fears have in common the fantasy of "bad" coming from the mother, with the child as the innocent victim who is about to be devoured, starved, drained, choked, and so on. Unless they are emotionally disturbed, mothers do not respond to their children in such cruel ways. Nevertheless, these fears seem real to the baby. In this manner, the prospect of refusal and deprivation become implanted in the child's unconscious mind and may haunt him for the rest of his life.

To preserve the feeling of being all-powerful, the child discovers an ingenious device. He sells himself on the idea that misery is his own doing, that he is in charge of it. Unconsciously he feels, "Others don't control me, I control them. Others don't reject me, I reject them." The child preserves his feeling of power by pretending that what the parents are making him do is really what he wanted to do in the first place: "I am the one who chooses to clean my room." The child makes the rules and regulations handed down by his parents appear to be his own, and thereby saves face and avoids the "insult" of parental demands. From 24 to 30 months of age, the child absorbs and incorporates the parent's rules and preserves his pride through the claim that he himself, of his own volition, abstains from forbidden actions.

If, for instance, he refrains from throwing his supper plate on the kitchen floor, he perceives it as a decision based entirely on his own judgment. He conveniently forgets that mother scolded him or even swatted him for doing it in the past. Children can also maintain their illusion of power by being naughty and making their parents punish or refuse them: "I made Mommy hit me; I caused her to reject me." Thus, a child may attempt to take back the power by provoking his caretakers to mistreat him even more.

Eventually, as the child grows, he transfers his illusion of being all-powerful over to his parents and teachers. In adolescence, he sees them as the ones who are all-powerful and assume a god-like status in his eyes.

Piaget reported that children, because of egocentrism or the attachment to the illusion of being all-powerful, are unable to understand another person's point of view. In the child's mind, the whole world revolves around him, and actions on the part of others are considered a result of his being or doing. Children personalize everything. Just as people of the Middle Ages believed the sun revolved around the earth, children believe that everything in their world revolves around them. A child in a park, for instance, runs over enthusiastically to pet a cat he sees. But the cat runs away, and the child exclaims to his mother, "Mom, the cat doesn't like me!" Or if Mom is depressed, he feels she must be mad at him.

As the child grows, his conscious mind covers over this primitive element. Nevertheless, as an adult he continues to take personally all kinds of reactions and responses from others. He takes it personally and feels rejected if a woman (instead of the cat) spurns his advances, although this woman might have been in a mood to spurn anyone's advances.

The child believes, Piaget wrote, that his thoughts have the power to change events and that things exist for his benefit. He credits the inanimate world with feelings like his own. He is sold on the cause and effect interpretation of life. If a child's mother says she has a headache and asks the child to leave her alone for a few minutes, the child may not be able to understand her point of view. The child may assume he is responsible for the headache, or he may feel rejected and unwanted by her need to be left alone. Some children will persist in pestering the mother until she gets mad. Adults assume that this annoying persistence indicates that the child is selfish or insensitive. But he simply is unable to consider any viewpoint but his own.

Learning to share, taking turns, listening to others while they are talking, and accepting another's point of view depend on the attainment of certain intellectual operations. The child is unable to grasp the idea of gratitude until adolescence when she can mentally and emotionally understand the concept.

To all this may be added a new ingredient: the feeling of displacement should a new brother or sister arrive. Ambivalent feelings of affection and dislike for each other are common among young siblings. These feelings persist into adulthood to be transferred onto other people. An older child may feel that her younger sibling deprives her of adequate nourishment and affection, even though she still gets these needs met by her mother. A child may be overwhelmed with feelings of rage and fantasies of destroying the little usurper. She feels dethroned, reduced, cast aside, deprived, and rejected. She casts jealousy upon the sibling and holds a grudge against her mother who she feels has betrayed her. She may act out, throw tantrums, or reject food and fun to protest the alleged deprivation and betrayal.

As the child stews in feelings of rejection and

deprivation, she develops a craving for acknowledgement and affection that allows no sharing whatsoever. This forms the foundation for jealousy, greediness, and unfairness that so many adults express. Now husbands, wives, friends, coworkers, and colleagues become the sibling rivals, threatening to take away her "cookies," leaving her feeling starved, rejected, and abandoned.

Three Major Stages of Human Development

Bergler wrote that the child is influenced by three primary self-defeating patterns, each of which is activated in successive psychosexual stages of development. The major link between all three phases is the feeling of being passively victimized. The child's life is steeped in complete dependence on his mother and her care. All of his misconceptions (baby fears) are a result of passive experiences in which he feels himself to be a victim. This is why the baby cannot distinguish "outer reality" from what he believes or perceives to be "outer reality."

First stage: "I want it and I want it now." The first stage, the oral stage, covers the first eighteen months of a child's life. In this stage, the child believes that the world is centered in himself (oneness), and that others are mere extensions of himself. Feeling dependent and helpless, the child becomes preoccupied with the idea of *not getting* (refusal, denial, deprival). The infant crying in his crib for milk that is not forthcoming immediately begins to experience the feeling of *not getting*. If the child feels he is everything and that others are extensions of himself, how does he account for the fact that some experiences are painful?

To resolve the problem, he takes credit for bringing upon himself the feeling of *not getting* or being deprived. He feels that he must have wanted this experience. How otherwise, given his conviction of omnipotence, could it possibly be happening to him? "I may be deprived and

199

denied," the child deduces, "but at least I'm doing it to myself." Now, deep down within, the child is able to "sugar-coat" the feeling of not getting and preserve his pride. This rationale sets in motion the propensity, in the later life of an adult, to feel refused, denied, deprived, and abandoned.

The consequences later in life of a fixation in the oral stage involve feelings of impatience, being easily let down, and the impulse to overdo in activities or with food, drink, sex, and work. This adult becomes addicted to the feeling of never having enough. He does not feel satisfied with what he has and develops a driving compulsion to satisfy, or have others satisfy, his every wish. He clings to the demand for exclusiveness. For example, a child asks his mother for candy. She refuses. This experience of being refused is repeated over and over again in various contexts. In time, the child begins to perceive the mother as a "great disappointer." He grows up into an adult who spends energy in emotional dramas of being disappointed and refused by those close to him as well as by life in general.

The second stage: "Who is going to control this situation?" The next phase, from eighteen months to three years, involves the child's period of early socialization and toilet training. The major feelings during this period are ones of being dominated, humiliated, controlled, and told to perform as expected. The child again feels overwhelmed by something more powerful than himself. To counter his passive feelings, he can become stubborn and refuse to produce, thereby upsetting his mother.

This is the period of "twoness" when the child experiences the other (mother) as separate from himself. This is the all-or- nothing stage, the birthplace of power conflicts, the beginning of win-lose, right and wrong. The following attitudes develop from this period: "It's either you or me." "If you shine, then I'm no good." "If I'm good, then you're bad." "If Mom is good, then Dad is bad." "If you win, then I lose." "If I'm right, then you're wrong."

The child is unable to accept two goods at the same time or any gray zones. Everything is black or white. Situations are seen in terms of who wins and who loses. "If I get my way, then I win." "If I have to do what you want, then I lose." One client told me her six-year-old son repeatedly came up to her and said, "You like Daddy more than me." Other times he said of the book she was reading, "You like that book more than me." She tried to explain to him that Mommy loved everyone in the family, but he saw it as either-or.

The child during this period is torn between the two feelings: caring and needing his mother versus perceiving her as bad in the sense of being restrictive, demanding, and depriving.

In this period, ambivalence appears, along with indecision, stubbornness, doubt, and uncertainty. If one thing is chosen, the other is missed. The child counters the experience of passive victim by becoming an active doubter or by being indecisive. Adults fixated at this stage show traits of indecisiveness, stubbornness, and righteousness. They become rigid, unyielding, unable to let go, and hold onto grievances to their own detriment. They tend to see reality as squashing them and controlling them. Consequently, there will always be a person or force (like a disease, an addiction or a job) that dominates them, and which they feel forces them to give up their own desires and makes them do what they do not want to do. To counter this attraction to being oppressed, they develop a compulsive drive to control everything.

The third stage: "Nobody loves me and nobody cares."
Finally, in this last stage, from about three to five years, the passivity is countered by exclusive love fantasies

toward the opposite-sexed parent. But since the parent is not available exclusively to the child, the child feels rejected, unloved, unwanted, betrayed, and abandoned. This is the time of two's company, three's a crowd ("threeness"), when the child feels like an outsider with the parents or the family and feels left out or pushed out of the picture. This is also the time when the child is sensitive to feeling degraded, shamed, criticized, and defeated in competition with others.

These feelings are countered by the need to be special, different, or have special powers. Emphasis is on performance ("see how good I am") and winning approval through pleasing, being good, or entertaining. Underneath, however, the child can become attached to the belief that he is never good enough, smart enough, or attractive enough. Inadequacy becomes the driving force behind his accomplishments. This period also gives rise later in life to the notorious triangle situations in relationships.

Is Perfect Parenting Possible?

Because of egocentrism and misunderstandings that form during these three stages of development, children tend to take personally their parents emotional reactions or corrections. They feel their parents do not give them enough and that they give more to others. They feel they never get enough attention, recognition, or praise. No matter what the child is given, he may be inclined to focus on what he did not get. In many cases, continually giving in to the child and trying to satisfy his every wish creates more insatiability in him.

These feelings and reactions are experienced even when parents do give adequate attention and affection. Naturally, if parents are not emotionally responsive, the child feels even more justified in feeling shortchanged. As mentioned, even under the best conditions, children are sensitive to indications of rejection, deprivation, or abandonment. And because of early dependence and helplessness, most children rebel at being restricted or confined. As I've said, there is no way that parents, even ideal parents, can cushion reality for the child so that he does not experience some degree of deprivation, oppression, or rejection.

Here is an example of a childhood misunderstanding that had damaging repercussions in adult years. Nate was born into a well-off professional family. He had private music lessons, tennis instruction, and most anything else he wanted. Nate's mother was raised in poverty with an alcoholic father who never gave her any affection or attention. Her mother, Nate's grandmother, was hard-working, yet passive to the demands and needs of her husband. Nate's mother vowed never to be like her mother, and she made the decision to give to her children all the attention and support that she never received as a child.

When Nate was born, she breast-fed him on demand, made his food from scratch, and showered him with attention and care. She wanted to make sure Nate never experienced the same fears, hurts, and inadequacies that she went through in childhood. She gave him ample support to get good grades and to excel at whatever he chose to do.

Yet, Nate perceived his mother's efforts and attempts to help him as evidence that he was inadequate because he apparently needed so much help from her. In his mind, the fact that his Mom helped him to read and do his homework meant that he was not capable of doing it on his own. He believed something was wrong with him. He interpreted his mother's generosity and love as an indication of his inability to succeed on his own.

Later in life, Nate interpreted any corrections made by teachers, girlfriends, or co-workers as criticism and an indication of his alleged inadequacies. He managed to sabotage his professional career because he felt he was not good enough and would not succeed. In his marriage, any comment, request, or feedback from his wife became further evidence of his alleged inadequacies. Yet, he depended upon his wife's advice and suggestions. Nate buried himself under the belief that he could not handle his life on his own and that he could not do anything right.

During stage three, the developing child's egocentrism is further assaulted by parental punishment and reproaches for naughtiness and stubbornness. Guilt, moral reproach, and punishment convince the typical child of the wisdom of acquiescing to his parents. An inner conscience is eventually built up in the psyche, followed by inner guilt. Meanwhile, the child's passive feelings about being refused and controlled are often shifted as aggressive reactions onto pets, dolls, siblings, or playmates.

Some children, however, cling to this fury against parental authority, provoking punishment. They coat the feeling of being punished with a feeling of excitement. Ten-year-old Bobby stubbornly refused to obey his parents, even though he knew punishments would be forthcoming. Rather than clean his room or be kind to his sister, he refused to do the work and continued to browbeat his sister. After each infraction, he was scolded and sent to his room without supper. There were times when he simply would not settle down until he had aroused his parent's wrath. "I swear," his mother said in exasperation, "that he did this to get us to come down on him. He set himself up for it." Indeed, Bobby did unconsciously set himself up to be punished and rejected.

This game of provoking punishment continued into adulthood. As a graduate student nearing the completion of his degree, he blurted out an obscenity to a professor who had denied some request. He was dropped from the program. Having provoked his punishment, Bobby felt unjustly victimized, rejected, and refused, as he had as a child.

The attachments to feeling controlled and rejected, and the feeling of having caused these experiences, take place below the conscious level. Consciously, individuals such as Bobby want love, approval, and success. But covertly they create rejection, disapproval, and failure. These negative feelings are unconsciously self-chosen, self-created, and self-maintained. On the surface, meanwhile, the individual feels self-pity and clings to the belief that he is an innocent victim of someone else's cruelty or negligence.

Many adults have a difficult time accepting the notion of the unconscious mind, recognizing its power, and seeing how it controls their behaviors. This is because it is equated with the power and "tyranny" of their parents in childhood. Feeling uncomfortable in admitting to being passively controlled by unknown forces within themselves, individuals much prefer to proclaim the power of their own decisions. "I, through my own greed, am responsible for my unhappiness," or "It's my jealousy that's caused me all this pain," or "I, because of my own inadequacies, failed to become what I intended to be." These admissions counter feelings of guilt and of being passively victimized, but they become instruments of the person's own defeat.

Our feelings and behaviors are the result of a combination of circumstances that include a) genetic endowments; b) resolution of conflict over childhood passivity and helplessness; c) clinging to childhood egocentrism and other misconceptions; d) degrees of self-reproach and self-aggression; and e) effects of parental attitudes, beliefs, and behaviors.

In the next chapter, I explore in more depth the effects of parental attitudes and behaviors on the development of emotional catering patterns and how these patterns persist in the adult.

Chapter 12
The Effects of Parenting

ECS Creed:
- Remember that you and only you are responsible for family morale and your parents' wellbeing. It is your job to make things better and make sure your parents are happy.
- Never think or say anything bad about your parents or how they raised you. Parents are always right.
- Resist truth or insight into yourself. Pretend that everything is wonderful.
- Blind yourself to your innermost feelings and let other people direct your life.
- Take it as a personal insult that other people refuse to own up to their faults

A child's tendency to claim power for what happens to him and to believe he causes his parents' reactions later emerges in the adult as emotional catering. The child's tendency to take responsibility and blame for events and situations is a way he or she defends against feelings of helplessness, powerlessness, rejection, and emotional deprivation. This strategy is an extension of the child's egocentrism or the illusion of being all-powerful: "Only I can manage this situation and make everyone feel better."

A child tries to reverse those uncomfortable feelings of dependency and emotional abandonment by becoming a parent to his own parents. He does this by taking on responsibility for the family morale and his parents' happiness. "I am not dependent on parents who abandon me and neglect me," his defense contends. "On the contrary, they are the ones who are dependent on me and need me to be happy." This role-reversal allows the child to suppress the pain of the domination and emotional neglect, whether real or perceived, he experiences in connection with his parents and siblings.

Becoming a parent to his parents diminishes the terror of being dependent on what the child perceives as emotionally insensitive parents who neglect or mistreat him. This reversal also serves to repair the narcissistic insult of having to be passively dependent on (and submit to) people he does not trust or who he perceives as not having his best interests at heart.

When a parent is unable to respond to his child in a sensitive loving manner, the child does not see this as a problem with the parent. Since the child believes he causes everything (egocentricity), he deduces that something is wrong with himself to account for the parent's insensitivity. He assumes that he is to blame. The child grows up compensating for his alleged inadequacies by trying to prove his fitness in his parent's eyes.

In addition to the usual dose of childhood egocentrism, fears, and disappointments, many emotional caterers had chaotic childhoods and recall feelings of being dependent on parents they perceived to be out of control. This out-of-control behavior includes parents' alcohol abuse, depression, compulsive behaviors, and narcissistic self-absorption. Regardless of the pattern, the child felt powerless to have a beneficial effect on his parents' behavior. He had no choice but to endure passively the parents' weaknesses. In such moments, the child perceived the parents as indifferent to him and unwilling to recognize him as a person in his own right. He perceived the parents to be absorbed with themselves and oblivious to any negative consequences their behaviors may have on him.

Having felt ignored as a child, the caterer believes he

is not worthy of attracting positive attention. In fact, he can become confused when someone praises him. He may even believe that something is wrong with him for drawing attention to himself or show disdain for people who recognize him.

For the child, love and validation were only experienced when he served, obeyed, or gave of himself to his parents. As long as the child performed according to parental expectations—never challenging the parents' behavior, never demanding anything for himself—love and approval would be forthcoming. The child learned to associate love with being needed. Selfless giving and serving, the child is convinced, result in getting love. On the unconscious level, however, the caterer has not recovered from feelings of being emotionally used and exploited in childhood.

As a child, the caterer took responsibility and blame for the parents' behavior to avoid feeling powerless and at the mercy of others who did not have her best interests at heart. Taking on the blame gave the child a pseudo-feeling of being in control. She took it on herself to provide for the emotional stability she felt lacking in the family. The need to control, fix, take care of, and arrange her life to please her parents became essential to avoid her feelings of being passively dominated, rejected, and emotionally starved.

Because these underlying feelings have not been acknowledged or resolved, the adult looks for or perceives similar forms of emotional neglect, deprivation, and control in her relationships. Typically, a caterer chooses someone who she eventually comes to perceive as needy, possessive, and dependent, and she repeats the same catering behavior she adopted with her parents, triggering off the same emotional hurts.

Because of this symbiotic enmeshment, caterers have a hard time leaving the "weak, needy other." There is no boundary between their own self and the self of the other person. As they identify so strongly with needy partners, they vicariously slip into their skins and feel their pain. A weak, needy partner represents the needy inner child the caterer does not want to acknowledge in herself. To be weak or needy is to bring forth feelings of being abandoned, unwanted, and shamed.

Leaving a spouse, firing an employee, or detaching from a needy friend or relative is analogous to abandoning and rejecting one's parents. The caterer is convinced she will be rejected and hated if she does not assist in managing the lives of others and saving them from themselves. As a child, she perceived that if she did not conform, agree with, and serve the needs of her parents she would be rejected and hated by them. The caterer is also convinced that to stop her catering behavior will devastate the parent (or other).

Self-Denial: Cornerstone of Catering

Joy, age thirty-six, was dissatisfied in her marriage to a 55- year-old man with numerous health problems. Her husband was attentive to her but she found him needy and suffocating. Their sexual relationship was nonexistent. He followed her around like a puppy, begging for attention. She felt restricted and trapped by her husband's emotional dependency, but feared that leaving him would destroy his life.

Suspecting that Joy's relationship with her husband mirrored her relationship with her dependent mother, I asked Joy to write a letter to her mother (for therapeutic use only) expressing how Joy felt about her childhood. Joy wrote:

> Dear Mother,
> I felt sorry for you for most of my life. I know you had a hard life and a difficult childhood. I really

wanted to fix it for you and make you happy. I cleaned the house and took care of the other kids hoping that it would make you happy. I thought that if you became happy we could spend some time together. I spent a lot of my childhood wondering what I could do to make you happy. Now I see it was a lost cause because it did not make you happy. I tried so hard to please you that there wasn't time to think about me. I have never figured out what would make me happy. If I never got it right for you, how could I get it right for myself. I felt like a failure for not being able to make you happy. If I failed the one person in life who I loved the most, then I am a failure and don't deserve anything.

You taught me that my purpose in life was to serve, work hard, and not to expect anything for myself. You taught me how to take care of you but not to take care of myself and give to myself the things that would make me happy. You taught me how to hide from real problems by losing myself in insignificant tasks and focusing all my energy on accomplishing the chores on my list.

I wish you had liked yourself enough to have not needed me so much. I can only be sorry that your childhood was so bad and wish that you could have found real help.

Joy's mother had been sick for most of Joy's childhood. As a child, Joy spent most of her time attending to her mother's needs and carrying out chores. Joy assumed the role of making sure Mom would survive and be happy. She acted out this same role with her husband. By focusing on his possible collapse into depression should she leave him, Joy buried her own feelings of being neglected, deprived, and abandoned. She used her fear of her husband's potential collapse as an excuse to remain in the catering position and perpetuate the self-denial that had become so familiar to her. Actually, she was terrified of being on her own, particularly without someone who needed her or depended on her. She was at a loss how to be herself without someone attached to her.

Joy was finally able to take time for herself, express her true feelings, and establish the kind of life she wanted for herself. This transformation evolved as she understood how she transferred her unresolved issues with her mother onto her husband and recreated the same self-neglect and denial she experienced in her childhood. Her husband improved in his ability to take care of himself and become more independent once Joy no longer babied him and catered to him.

Self-denial is the cornerstone of emotional catering. Without the attachment to self-denial, the whole pattern collapses. Over the many years of childhood, the child becomes accustomed to relative degrees of emotional deprivation. In caterers, the experience of *not getting* becomes so powerful that even when emotional support is offered, the individual does not or cannot absorb it. The caterer is convinced emotionally that nothing of value can come from his caretakers, and that the only way to get anything is to give it to himself. Thus, he embarks on a determined course of self-sufficiency and responsibility. The aim is to avoid being put in a position of dependency on others who he believes will let him down or not give to him the love and nurturing he desires. But the situation he tries so desperately to avoid is what he is conditioned to repeat. He ends up taking care of himself and others while getting little in return.

As mentioned, the caterer hides his self-denial by giving to others what he felt was never given to him, in a defense called a magic gesture. "You see, Mom and Dad, how I give to others," the unconscious defense contends.

"Unlike you, I would never abandon or crush someone in their time of need. If only you had been as loyal and giving to me as I have been to others."

The magic gesture is a reversal of what the child experienced with his parents. In this way, he betters the parents, yet his supposedly altruistic behavior leaves the caterer feeling bitter and rejected when his "giving" is not reciprocated. The more the caterer gives and does not get back, the more he flirts with the bittersweet feeling of being neglected and abandoned by his parents, recycling buried feelings of hurt and abandonment he had with them.

The Great Law

Marsha had written a letter to her father to get in touch with buried feelings towards him. She wanted to understand how her relationship with him had influenced her feelings toward her husband and herself. She did not intend to actually confront her father (he would likely have a completely different perspective on what happened in the past), but to heal the wounds and grievances that still persisted within herself. She wanted to understand more completely how she was living out the feelings, experiences, and beliefs that influenced her in the past. She wrote:

Dear Dad,

I wish that I had mattered more to you and that you had been more accepting of me. I remember hiding behind trees or staying in my room, quiet as a mouse, hoping that you would never find me so that I would not have to stand silent before you to receive your wrath. I remember being beaten with a branch from a tree that I was forced to cut and return to you for something I did not do. You beat me until you drew blood on the backs of my legs. I remember screaming and you telling me to shut up or you would beat me harder. I just kept screaming until I was too tired. I remember thinking that I would scream louder and louder to show you. I wanted to hurt you like you were hurting me.

All my childhood you tormented me and judged me on the basis of what your other children did. When I was fifteen you called me vile names and accused me of being a whore. I was a virgin until I was twenty and I wondered why you called me a tramp. I was badly bruised by your judgments. In retaliation, I was cruel and unkind to the young men who pursued me. I always ran away when a nice man liked me and tried to get close to me. I felt like I was a bad person anytime someone liked me or showed kindness towards me.

I was an overachiever to make up for the voids that were too overwhelming in my life. You taught me well, Dad, that hardness and toughness were just a means to deny my needs and my feelings and a way to protect me from reality. You taught me not to receive love but to push it away. To receive love meant I was a bad person unworthy of feeling good.

I wish you could have held me and told me that you loved me, and that I was a neat and wonderful person who could achieve and enjoy all the good loving things in life. I wish you had told me that I was deserving of love, of feeling love, and giving love. I wish that you could have had the foresight and the education to deal with a child like me. I had visions and worth that had to be denied because I realized early on that you could not deal with my mind, my knowledge, or the strong will that I possessed. I always felt superior to you, yet the child in me could not be irreverent to my parent.

I suppose somewhere along the line you taught me respect—yet it was respect earned the wrong

*way and the hard way. All my life I have done things
the long and hard way. I have the work ethic
ingrained in my head to the point of being a
workaholic, which is a product of your judgments. I
can and do forgive you for this, as I know you
meant well, and I know because of your dysfunction
that you never realized what you did to me. It is
now up to me to heal the wounded child within and,
as I cry in tears of sadness and emptiness, I realize
I am now on the road to healing.*
Love, Marsha

Marsha had been married to a difficult man for thirty
years. Her husband was unable to tolerate complaints,
criticisms, or frustration of his desires, and he degraded
her by being verbally abusive. According to Marsha, he
had to have his way at all costs. Everything was focused
on her husband and his needs. No attention was given to
her feelings or needs. Whatever she did for him, it was
never good enough. Marsha had been suppressing her
true feelings about her husband for many years, fearing
his wrath and anger. But now she could no longer hold
herself back. She was torn by the conflict between being
herself, expressing the truth of what she felt, and the fear
that her husband would "demolish" her.

"Was your father in some ways like your husband?" I
asked Marsha.

"There are differences in their surface personalities,
but they are the same in their demand for total
compliance and allegiance. There was never any thought
of challenging my father, talking back to him, or
confronting him with what I felt. I believed he would hurt
me severely or banish me if I challenged him in any way.
I had to ignore his cruelty and insensitivity and pretend he
was wonderful. I had to like his mistreatment. I feel the
same way with my husband."

As children, Marsha and others like her enter into unconscious agreements or silent pacts with their parents. The terms of this pact require the child to overlook and to refrain from challenging perceived abuse, lies, or other forms of emotional insensitivity. The child feels forced to go along with what the parents are doing, affirm the parents' opinions, and never criticize their behavior.

One client remarked, "I felt that I would be killed if I ever dared to challenge my father's behavior or opinions." She described the atmosphere in her childhood: "It was like being in a snake-pit. You didn't dare move, say anything, or show any life. You had to remain rigid, silent, and endure, or you would be bitten. It was total terror."

In her adult life, this woman had a difficult time expressing her true feelings. Emotionally, she was still in the snake-pit.

The child's withholding of contrary feelings and perceptions is taken as acceptance and "love" by his parents. To earn that "love," the child must pretend that he does not see or know what is happening in the family. The child is not supposed to see or discuss Mother's bouts of depression or Dad's irrational anger attacks. The child must keep quiet, obey, and discount his own perceptions of what he sees.

Like a crooked accountant who confirms that the books are okay when they are not, the child goes along with the lies and deceptions. As time goes on, the child eventually comes to believe that the family dysfunction is "normal." This is because children unconsciously borrow patterns of misery and self-defeat from their parents. With parents as their primary models, children give their parents a supreme authority that makes parental behaviors and reactions appear normal.

This unconscious agreement to aid and abet the inner corruption of the family dysfunction occurs at a high cost to the child. The child has no choice but to buy into the belief system of the family. If Dad says he is not drunk (even though he's tottering about the house), then he is not drunk. Drunken behavior becomes normal parental behavior to the child.

Many parents unconsciously attempt to use a child to meet their own emotional needs. The child is expected to be there for them, agree with them, and never talk back. The child can also be used by a parent to protect and defend the parent's own system of denial. The child feels that no identity is allowed outside of this emotional, dependent conspiracy. He must accept this strangling bond of blind complicity to aid in protecting the parents or he will be hated and abandoned.

Mary recalled an incident that illustrates this predicament. Her mother had been away from home for a few weeks, and when she returned Mary told her that father had been drunk and abusive towards her. In a rage, her father said Mary was making up the story to make him look bad and that she was crazy to make such false accusations against him. He promised dire consequences if she ever "lied" about him again and made her apologize for the incident. She remembered feeling responsible and guilty for what had happened and believed it was all her fault.

Mary's mother did not stand up to her husband's drinking, violent rages, and mistreatment of the children. Instead, her mother made excuses for him: "Try to understand Dad," mother would say, "he has a drinking problem and he can't help it. He would not be so mean if he didn't have a drinking problem."

Her mother's protection of her husband made Mary feel sorry for him and encouraged her to imitate her mother's passivity. It also encouraged her to overlook her father's deficiencies. Like her mother, she believed she was being a good girl by "suffering" through her father's problems. Mary felt she had no choice but to bear the cost of her mother's passivity by allowing herself to be shamed and humiliated by her father. In her marriage, she recreated her mother's pattern of protecting the male by taking the blame for her husband's irrational and insensitive behavior.

As she had done with her father, Mary passively agreed to accept her husband's behavior in an attempt to ensure he would love her. She believed that if she stood up to her husband and refused to go along with his behavior, her relationship would suffer. It was *either* betray her father (now her husband) *or* be used and betrayed by him. Mary expressed it this way, "I felt I had to give up my opinions and feelings to fill his needs. I was not enough as I was; I had value only when I was useful or when I could do things for him."

When a child feels forced to keep silent and is not allowed to express her feelings about insensitive patterns in the family, she will lack the ability as an adult to see through people's behavior and avoid being easily conned. She will believe the most blatant lies. She will not trust her own perceptions, having been trained to go along with the prevailing view or rely on other's interpretations and opinions. She will blind herself to the flaws and weaknesses of others and set herself up to be taken advantage of and seduced. She will even blind herself to the truth about her own needs and feelings because she believes it is bad to see truth or to discuss it. She will be afraid to question her colleagues or authority figures and will avoid taking risks in her career, fearing that she will be destroyed if she should challenge the prevailing view.

Many children feel their parents never allowed them to have negative thoughts or feelings. Their parents expected them to be happy, even when the children did not feel it. Such children grew up believing it was important to make the parents feel good by denying any negative feelings. Some children grow up adopting an

217

optimistic cloud of phony happiness, thinking that this attitude validates their parents' lives. But this positive facade is not real; it obscures what they honestly feel and experience. This is how children can lose touch with themselves.

In a situation where the child is recruited to validate or deny the family dysfunction, the child anticipates that her feelings and beliefs will be ignored and neglected by others. She also learns to ignore and neglect her own feelings. She gives up her own perceptions of reality and conforms to what others want. She concludes that her perceptions of reality are wrong and that she must be crazy to see things so differently. As an adult, she automatically submits to the perceptions and views of others. She does not expect other people to listen to her or take her seriously. She assumes that her feelings and viewpoints will be discounted and turned against her. She believes what others say about her, even when she knows it might not be true.

A client described the effect of having her own reality denied by her mother. "Mother's version of reality was that friends are bad, boys are bad, bodies are bad, kids are dumb, parents are smart, and that wanting things for yourself is selfish," she said. "I adopted her version completely and consequently did not seek out friends or male relationships. I hated my body and acted dumb. I felt guilty anytime I wanted something for myself and could not allow myself to get anything expensive." This woman continued to experience as an adult the course her mother had charted for her.

In their adult relationships, caterers adopt the same helpless and powerless attitude with others they once adopted with their parents. They feel threatened when challenging others. They feel threatened with the prospect of being unloved or abandoned should they be genuine and speak the truth of what they feel. To the child, being good and loving her parents means validating their words and behavior. As an adult, loving someone still means validating and accepting without question the other person's behavior.

Because she had to blind herself to the obvious as a child, the adult caterer does not see or take action when it is in her best interest to do so. She resists truth and insight into herself because truth is "bad," as it was in childhood. As an adult, she now identifies with her parents who denied their character flaws. Like Mom and Dad, she now pretends that everything is as it should be. She loses the ability to see into her own negative flaws and consequently denies her irrational behavior, as her parents once did. She is blind to the truth in herself as well as in others. To see herself is interpreted as bad and shameful.

Many caterers feel resistant to getting help. Unconsciously, they identify with their parents who were also reluctant to face their emotional problems. Like her parents, the caterer does not want others to see into her flaws and weaknesses. Imitating her parents, she seeks only sympathy for her suffering rather than the truth that could free her. When it would serve her best interest to see and understand, she resists and blinds herself to innermost feelings: "I'm just doing what Mom and Dad taught me to do. They taught me it was bad to see these things."

As an adult, she puts blind trust in others who are not worthy of trust and fails to trust those who are worthy. She becomes loyal to people who mistreat her or take advantage of her, recreating her experience with her parents. She goes along with whatever truth or reality is promoted by others and sets herself up to be easily exploited. Under these conditions, she cannot see objectively.

The caterer abdicates personal decision-making. Even

if she has doubts, she concedes that, "This is the way things are. Who am I to know better?" Because the conscious aim is to secure approval and love, the caterer does not direct an effective challenge to a bully or tyrant. She becomes absorbed into the prevailing belief system.

Because of the silent pact made with their families, emotional caterers fear going against the prevailing viewpoint in their personal interactions and in society in general. They follow mainstream ideas and hesitate to enter into areas of creative controversy where they might be criticized or challenged. They lose their ability to critique the policies of those governing them and blindly follow other people's perspectives. This tendency dampens creative outflow. They avoid taking the risks needed to advance themselves, thereby maintaining their sense of boredom and failure.

Watching Others Get Away with It

Some individuals raised under terms of the Great Law feel hurt or insulted when they see others get away with "misbehaviors." They have a compelling need to hold others accountable for "corrupt" or inappropriate behavior. These individuals take the refusal of others to acknowledge faults as a personal injustice and betrayal.

Marianne, a business manager, was furious that a less competent colleague was promoted over her. It simply was not fair. Marianne had struggled daily in the trenches to get where she was, and she resented others who were rewarded without having to do the same degree of hard work. She had also been complaining for years that her husband got away with not doing as much housework as she did. Both Marianne and her husband had full-time jobs, but Marianne's husband came home and took naps before dinner. "How come he can get away with taking naps and shirking his responsibilities? If I tried that, I'd really get it. It just isn't fair," she exclaimed.

Marianne became riled at criminals who "got away" with their crimes and corporations that "got away" with taking advantage of the public. She was entrenched in the mentality that others were always taking away her benefits and getting away with it. In the meantime, she felt helpless, degraded, and deprived, with no control over these circumstances.

As a child, she grew up with two younger brothers close to her age. She was jealous of their closeness with her mother. In her eyes, her bothers had been favored and got away with things without being punished. As Marianne saw it, "How come he gets away with being naughty, but I always get caught and punished?" She also perceived that her brothers got a bigger share of the dessert (which also represents the "breast" or mother), and did not have to do as much around the house.

It seemed to her that her parents had never let her get away with anything. If she wanted to go out, she had to finish her chores first. If she left something undone, her father had roused her from sleep to make her finish her task. As a teenager, she took risks by staying out too late and coming home after drinking too much. Naturally, she got caught, which convinced her that she was always the one who was scolded and punished while her brothers got away with their misbehaviors.

Marianne's father was alcoholic. He denied his drinking problem and resisted any attempt to reform his behavior. When he drank, he was frequently verbally abusive. No one in the family was allowed to make any protest about this abuse. They were expected to endure it and pretend everything was normal. Marianne saw her father "getting away" with his corrupt behaviors. It irked her that he was never held accountable, nor ever admit he was being hurtful and insensitive.

As an adult, she secretly kept this grudge alive. She feasted on opportunities to feel like a passive victim to others whom she perceived as "getting away with things." This could take the form of a devious or cruel person getting away with his misbehavior or a lazy person taking the easy way out. From her perspective, power and privilege were always in someone else's hands. She could only watch someone else enjoy getting the benefits while she felt starved. Or someone else was always stealing the show.

She colluded in this experience by passively sitting back and watching others get or by failing to fully pursue her aspirations, thereby intensifying the feeling of being neglected, overlooked, and unappreciated. If Marianne really valued her own achievements, there would be no need for her to suffer when she saw less competent others get the goodies.

The Need to Make Others Take Responsibility

Like Marianne, many of us become resentful and frustrated when others refuse to divulge the "truth" about themselves and own up to their wrongdoings. We personalize the defensive or self-protective behavior of other people. We take the refusal of another to take responsibility for his faults as a personal rejection of who we are, as well as a rejection of our ideas and values. We feel we cannot be validated unless others own up to their mistreatment of us. Needing the other to admit to his faults only serves to recycle feelings of being denied, betrayed, and rejected.

Some therapy circles encourage individuals to directly confront their parents with alleged mistreatments. Unfortunately, most of these efforts do not solve the person's problem. The more one tries to convince parents of their alleged "crimes," the more the parents find reasons to justify their behavior, especially if they feel guilty or inadequate. Such confrontations usually create more alienation because the parents and children have very different perspectives on the past. (Children have the tendency to elaborate on the hurt of parental neglect or oversight and to overlook the positive.) This type of confrontation can even increase the hurt if the parents have not come to terms with their own issues.

Most people cannot be honest with themselves. We do not lie or deny our misbehavior in order to hurt others. People do so to protect their self-image. Ask yourself, why does it bother you so much that someone else is not taking responsibility for himself or owning up to a fault? If the other fails to acknowledge your version of reality, how does that affect you?

One client replied: "If they acknowledge their stuff, then I don't have to feel guilty and responsible for them anymore. I will be free from worry and concern about their wellbeing." This answer revealed more about her. She was setting herself up to feel trapped and obligated by the unhappiness of others. She believed that if she were not there to take care of others, they would collapse and she would be abandoned.

Another client replied, "If they do not accept my version of reality, then I have to accept their version. It's an either-or situation." However, if you make your wellbeing dependent on someone else's honesty or admission of wrongdoing, you will go on recycling feelings of being betrayed, deprived, and cheated.

I often see people resist healthy behavior because they do not want (unconsciously) to give up feeling like victims of their parents' bungling. Some caterers cringe as they imagine one of their parents saying, "You see, son, look at you, you turned out great. We weren't bad parents after all."

Individuals can hold onto grievances with their parents by becoming failures or "emotional basket-cases." Becoming successful or happy feels like submission to the parents' will and validation of the correctness of their actions. If you fail, you can indeed make your parents look bad. You can contend, though at great personal cost to yourself: "You see what you did to me—I can't function in my life because of you, and I won't let you forget it."

Many caterers resist seeing the good in their parents. It feels to them like a loss of pride to accept love and goodness from their families. A caterer who has transformed his self-defeating behavior understands that his parents had good intentions, and that they may not have been conscious of how they reacted to him. Most parents believed they gave and responded appropriately, or at least did as well as they could. The caterer comes to understand that his parents, like himself, were also subject to the same infantile conflicts and misunderstandings.

Caterers must accept the emotional and physical reality of what happened to them in childhood. No person, situation, success, or financial gain can change what happened in the past. Making parents confess to their "crimes" or trying to change them into super-parents, will not remove old hurts. The solution is to accept what happened and learn how the old hurts are being maintained, mostly unconsciously, in the present.

Better parenting results when individuals work through their own childhood issues with their parents and connect with the wounds and grievances they are carrying over into their adult lives. Many parents are not aware of how they unconsciously transfer their emotional issues with their own parents onto their children. Parents also need to understand that they tend to treat their children in the same way they were treated as children. Unconsciously, they become a caricature of their parents and subject their children to what they endured.

For example, Dan, a businessman, frequently belittled his wife and children with harsh judgments. He expected them to wait on him immediately. Dan's father had behaved this way toward Dan, so Dan was unconsciously subjecting his family to the same treatment he had received. When he became aware of how he "became like" his father and how he had borrowed this judgmental pattern from his father, he began to change his behavior. He realized that this pattern of becoming like his dad was his way of denying and repressing the hurt and pain of feeling a victim of a father who mistreated him.

As parents, we also need to recognize that our children can exaggerate and misinterpret our corrections or actions. Once parents understand a child's tendency to ascribe negative intentions to their corrections, they will not be so tempted to take personally their child's resistant reactions.

The greatest gift you can give your children is to be a model of what you want your children to be. Children observe the choices you make, the freedoms and pleasures you allow yourself, the talents you have developed, and even the abilities you have ignored. You need to manifest in yourself those qualities, values, and emotional attitudes toward life that you want for your children.

Exercise
Write a separate letter to your mother and father, or to stepparents and siblings. This is a therapeutic letter and is not intended to be read by them. In the letter include:
1. How you felt as a child toward that parent (or sibling). Describe your relationship.
2. Describe each parent's strengths and weaknesses.
3. Describe how you believed your parents regarded you. How did your mother see you? How did your father see you? Have you treated yourself or others in the same manner? Example, "Dad saw me as a burden. I dragged him down and gave him nothing of value. I could do nothing right in his

eyes. Now I often see others as a responsibility and a burden. I, too, hold myself back and see little value in personal relationships. I can do nothing right in my own eyes."

4. How have your parents affected your life?
5. What would you have liked to have received from them? Or how would you have wanted them to respond to you?
6. List the ways you are like each parent and have expressed the same traits and feelings.
7. Express the grievances you are still holding against them and compare these feelings to feelings you may have now toward others in your life.
8. Become your parent and write a letter back to yourself. Write as your parent, describe your feelings, and give an interpretation of why you responded to yourself as a child in the way you did.

Chapter 13
Path to Emotional Independence

ECS Creed:
- Emotional health is impossible.
- Health is boring. What would I do if I did not have any grudges to nurse or emotional dramas to complain about?
- Things are not supposed to work out for me.
- If something good happens, some disaster will come along to take it away.
- I'm okay. It's others who need help.
- There is no such thing as happiness.

What can a person do once he recognizes the pattern of emotional catering? How does he learn to experience life more positively, manifest his dreams and aspirations, and feel free to be himself?

In this hi-tech world, we sometimes like action-oriented procedures that produce a quick fix. Most people want instant change with little effort and prefer not to see anything about themselves that is uncomfortable. This desire for immediate, painless change reflects more of an infantile need to be taken care of than a realistic understanding of psychological transformation.

The mentality of emotional caterers cannot be changed overnight. Changing long-standing negative habits requires training. But if you really want it, you will not be afraid to put in the time and the effort. Mastery of your emotions requires focused observation of your feelings and reactions. You can start by rereading the six features of catering in chapter 1 and identifying how you experience these patterns in your life.

While there are no short-cuts, the guidelines and techniques outlined in this chapter facilitate one's transformation.

Emotional Disturbances Originate in You

It is a fallacy to believe that emotional salvation lies outside yourself. To rely on others or outer circumstances to feel better or change your behavior puts you at the mercy of forces you cannot control. Waiting for another person to change so that you can feel better is an excuse to indulge in being a victim of that person.

The belief that we are innocent victims of someone else's mistreatment provides a built-in excuse for our failures, as well as a justification for not taking responsibility for our lives. When our happiness depends on our own perception of reality, rather than on the behaviors of others, then we have choices and options. We have the power to change. Liberation consists of insight into the ways we feel and perceive reality. It means relinquishing the victim perspective and "seeing" ourselves and others more objectively.

It is not so much what happens to us that causes us suffering, but how we interpret and react to what happens to us. It is true that we are affected and influenced by outside events and other people, yet our specific emotional reactions to these events are our choice. You are responsible for your emotional reactions even though others may be neglecting you or mistreating you.

The world is challenging and often unfair, so we will experience failures and disappointments. One of the hardest realities for us to handle is our feeling of helplessness concerning our circumstances. Why did the hurricane hit our town and not theirs? Why did I live and the other person die? Why did that person win the lottery and not me? We feel ourselves at the mercy of forces out of our control and powerless to do anything about it.

We sometimes counter these helpless feelings with magical thinking: "I've always had bad luck." "I wasn't blessed." "It happened because I've been bad." "This is a sign that I'm supposed to stay at this job."

It's hard for us to accept the randomness of fate without personalizing it. Furthermore, many of us have the expectation that reality should meet our needs instantly, or, in other words, give us the baby bottle without any effort on our part. These unrealistic expectations are remnants of the infantile mind.

Life itself is not bad; it is our perceptions and interpretations that make us miserable. Bad things do not occur specifically to make us suffer. It's true, we do have limited effect on others and the world. Still, we do have power over our own reactions and responses.

When we are under emotional stress, most of us want to run away, move, look for a new lover, attain more money, etc. These changes can produce a temporary high, a temporary escape from negative feelings. But a permanent feeling of wellbeing is dependent upon an "internal adjustment" in our emotional reactions. This internal adjustment is contingent upon a close examination of our negative feelings and perceptions.

Ask yourself: "How do you react to the world and how do you let it affect you? Do you blow everyday nuisances out of proportion or use the flaws of others to perpetuate disappointment?

Sit Still and Look at your Feelings

Rather than repress our negative perceptions and emotions, we must discover their origins. We do this by taking an honest inventory of our feelings about our relationships, our careers, our feelings towards ourselves, and our behaviors. We observe and understand our own emotional reactions rather than focus on what the other person is doing or not doing. Instead of analyzing the faults of others or what you feel they are doing to you, ask yourself, "What am I feeling right now? How am I letting this person make me feel? Why am I reacting this way? Why am I dissatisfied with myself or with this person?"

If you want to understand yourself, observe yourself like a scientist observing nature. Cultivate the position of being a non-critical observer of your reactions. Initially, you may find it hard to focus on your inner feelings since they have, to some degree, been blocked off since childhood. Keeping a journal in which you record your feelings is helpful. Each day write down the feelings you experienced. (Appendix B on "How to Define Your Feelings" is helpful.) Ask yourself, "What did I feel today? If you were angry with someone, ask yourself, "Why did I get angry with that person? What did I initially feel that caused me to get angry? Was I feeling ignored, insulted, or used?"

In order to free yourself, you need to reverse the process of blaming others. Blaming means you hold other people or circumstances responsible for your negative emotional reactions Energy is spent getting the alleged oppressor to own up to what he's done to you. Evidence of his injustice is gathered to prove your right to hold onto the hurt. Notice how addictive it is to feel a victim of people's mistreatment or inadequacies and how you want to hold them responsible for your misery.

For example, a person might say, "I reacted to my wife being late by feeling rejected and disappointed. I took her being late as an indication that I'm not important enough to her." People want to blame the other person for their reactions, claiming that, "If she hadn't been late, I wouldn't be so upset and hurt. She made me feel rejected. She let me down again." Remember, others don't usually cause you to feel a certain way. What typically happens is that you are quick to interpret their words or actions in a way that causes you pain and suffering.

The following four-step process can help you let go of long-standing resentments and grievances. Remember that the energy you tie up in hurts, anger, and resentments reduces the energy left for positive feelings or creative endeavors.

1. Identify the specific grievance you are holding onto and feel the emotions connected with it. If you feel angry, you need to understand the feelings beneath the anger. For example, anger is usually a reaction to negative emotions involving rejection, betrayal, denial, deprivation, criticism, or being controlled. Yet you are usually the one who is nursing those painful emotions.

2. Compare these feelings with the feelings and perceptions of your childhood. Ask yourself, where does this hurt come from in my past or what does this situation remind me of in my childhood? When have I experienced similar hurts? With whom? What am I recreating from my childhood experience? Keep in mind that you likely have repressed the original pain and hurt. Look in particular for emotional patterns that repeat themselves over and over. The purpose of this exercise is not to place blame but to understand how we transfer the same childhood feelings and perceptions onto our present relationships.

3. Confront your participation in your reactions. In the painful situation you might use as an example, ask yourself, "Did I collude in bringing about the grievance? For example, did I provoke the other person to respond negatively towards me?" (Lying, forgetfulness, picking fights, or a lack of cooperation are examples of provocations. So are nagging, criticizing, analyzing, or begging for reassurance.) Usually we are subtly provoking from others the very reactions we claim to hate.

Or ask yourself, "How am I like the person I am

having a problem with?" Are you projecting your own unwanted or uncomfortable traits onto others who are disturbing you? Are you expecting others to treat you as your parents treated you? Ask yourself, "Am I acting like my mother (or father) and subjecting others to what I received as a child?"

Consider any benefits for continuing to hold onto hurts or grievances, such as using them as excuses for failure or for getting others to give you attention.

4. Negative emotions dissipate naturally when we see and understand how we transfer hurtful feelings experienced in the past onto our present life circumstances. For example, Angie, a housewife, insisted her husband did not love her because he liked to look at other women and devote more energy to his hobbies than to her. Consequently, she felt inadequate and unattractive, and she wondered what she was doing to cause his lack of interest.

Her intense conviction of feeling unwanted and unimportant was traced back to her childhood relationship with her father. Angie's father was involved with different activities that took him away from home, and he had an affair when she was ten years old. Angie also perceived that her siblings got more attention from her father than she did. She felt unwanted and inadequate in his eyes.

In her adult life, she unconsciously looked for opportunities to feel ignored and not valued. She saw others (other women) getting more attention from her husband. In order to experience this old hurt, she even provoked her husband to ignore her with constant nagging.

She looked for "proof' that her perceptions about him were correct, thereby justifying her right to feel bad and unloved. Whether or not her husband was emotionally remote was not relevant to the resolution of Angie's pain.

She needed to see that she was eager to interpret his behavior as being against her so she could feel the old, unresolved hurt.

Demanding that her husband become more involved with her would not solve her insecurity about feeling unloved. Taking responsibility for her reaction to her husband did not mean that he was innocent and she was wrong. Taking responsibility meant acknowledging her willingness to use his behavior to feel unloved and unimportant.

Permanent transformation of negative feelings occurs only when we discover the historical origins of our negative feelings and acknowledge how attached we have become to them. When we acknowledge this attachment, we automatically become more positive towards ourselves and others, and have no need for positive affirmations. Insight now gives us the ability to make wise choices.

Self-improvement programs that use positive thinking or imagery believe you can change your behavior by imagining in your mind how you want to be. But visualization or imagery has little to do with behavior change. Changing our habits, negative emotions, or self-defeating behaviors depends primarily on an unconscious decision to change. Often, we attribute positive changes to books, techniques, or some self-improvement program when, in fact, change has happened because of an inner decision.

When a person has made an unconscious decision not to change, his use of positive imagery has limited application and produces only temporary results. For the most part, he is unaware of his inner resistance. On the conscious level, he rationalizes his failure, saying, "It's just too hard; this technique doesn't work." Most failures to change are due to the conviction that doing the right thing deprives us, hurts too much, or is just too much effort.

Self-help programs that promote the use of positive imagery and positive thinking have strong appeal because they give us a sense of control over our negative feelings and distressful circumstances. But all we achieve is an illusion of being in control. Even if such a program has some apparent benefit, it makes us dependent on something outside of ourselves to feel better. The program soon becomes the end in itself, acting like a tranquilizer that keeps our true motivations and inner needs hidden and repressed. Sometimes, we attach ourselves to new or "improved" programs when the original one loses its effectiveness.

In order to let go of negative feelings permanently, we need to understand that we interpret our lives and our relationships through the eyes of the child part of our psyche. Children are inherently self-centered and egocentric. They feel that the world and everyone in it is focused on them. They believe that everyone sees or should see reality the way they see it. They cannot understand that other people have different perspectives. This attitude persists into adulthood and causes conflict in our relationships. Rather than listen to others, we defend ourselves or try to prove our perceptions to be right. We jump to conclusions or negative assumptions rather than ask questions about how the other person interpreted what happened. It is this rigid self-centered way of thinking that causes us to feel diminished when others disagree with our perceptions or opinions.

Children are steeped in either-or consciousness. They feel that everything is either black or white, right or wrong, good or bad, for me or against me. When the child sees others get, he can feel deprived. If he doesn't win the prize, then he deduces he's a lesser person. The child cannot conceive of two goods or two rights at the same time, or even bad and good at the same time. We believed as children that we were supposed to be perfectly good, and if not then we were bad. Consequently, many of us take criticism as evidence we are flawed and unworthy. It's hard for us to conceive that negative and positive coexist, that the negative does not have to negate the positive.

Insight into how we maintain our child-centered perspective automatically causes a change in how we feel about ourselves, others, and life. When we can see objectively, we free ourselves to make clearer, centered decisions about what we should do or what changes will work to our best advantage. Gradually the old feelings and negative reproaches wither away and die, leaving in their place new found feelings of confidence, contentment, and serenity.

Retrieving Buried Emotional Wounds

No matter how negligent your parents might have been, you still have to take responsibility for the fact that, when in misery, you are making choices to react to life with negative expectations. Bad or abusive parenting certainly has a profound effect on the feelings and behaviors of the child. But you have the choice as an adult whether or not to maintain or keep alive your past hurts. Many people use the belief that "my parents ruined my life" to justify their pursuit of failure or deprivation. Holding a grudge against others only hurts you and blocks the possibility of inner peace.

As caterers retrieve past emotional hurts, they experience powerful feelings of sadness concerning the lack of caring and acceptance they believe they experienced in childhood. You might need to grieve consciously over this loss, to the extent it actually occurred, but understand that nothing can change the reality of your past. The key is to shift your focus from what *was* done to you to deeper understanding of how you *now* unwittingly deprive yourself and repeat the hurt in the present.

A child's feelings of being a victim can become more intense or pervasive in the adult. However, until we become more aware, it feels as if there is no choice but to respond emotionally in the same way we reacted as children. We have identified ourselves with feelings of being unloved, denied, and controlled. When we first let go of these feelings, we feel like we lose a sense of who we are. We see change as loss, not gain, and we fear losing ourselves in the process. We do not know how "to be" without being enmeshed in the old patterns.

Some authors and lecturers suggest the solution to health and happiness is in letting go of our resentments and forgiving those who have wronged us. This is not as easy as it sounds. Intellectually, we want to forgive, but the emotional part of our psyche has a totally different agenda. It wants to hold onto the gripes and grievances and resists letting them go. This resistance has to be understood and acknowledged.

Forcing forgiveness when it is not really felt emotionally or conjuring up positive images to cover up buried grudges are dead-end detours. Both techniques create inner resistance. It is awareness of the truth of one's negative feelings and how they play out in our present lives, along with insight and effort, that changes negative patterns.

I had a client who was "trying" to forgive his father. He wrote in a letter to his father, "I forgive you, Dad, for screwing me up." This statement indicated he still felt himself to have been a victim of his father's alleged mistreatment. Another client remarked, "I forgave my parents long before I even knew what I was forgiving." This was faked forgiveness, not genuine forgiveness.

When an individual understands how he unconsciously holds onto old hurts of feeling unloved, deprived, and somehow victimized, he ceases to blame his parents or others for his suffering. Consequently, he has nothing to forgive since there is no grudge. Forgiveness becomes a moot point once a person recognizes how he perpetuates the role of victim in his life by holding others responsible for his distress.

Rather than forgiveness, I see compassion and understanding as the key elements in transformation. Compassion means the ability to see both sides of an emotional stressful situation. You are capable of understanding the other person's point of view, though you may not agree with it, as well as understanding your emotional complicity in your reaction to that person. Compassion implies the ability to know and accept yourself with all your imperfections. Compassion means acceptance of what happened and of the way things happen.

To develop compassion, you must learn to listen to yourself and others in a totally new way. Compassion is kin to curiosity. You feel curious about how others feel or see things. You are curious about your own feelings and reactions. You care about the way others feel. You care about yourself and your feelings as well.

Do you really listen to what other people are saying? Do you listen to your partner, your children, to yourself? Do you carefully observe your feelings, fears, and negative thoughts? Or do you get caught up in your own rigid convictions and judgments of how you think things should be?

Ask yourself: "What would you feel if you discovered that your parents really did love you?" Notice any resistance to believing or feeling this. Observe how a part of you wants to see your parents as unloving and deficient. If you feel in conflict with a parent (or anyone), try imagining yourself in their position. Imagine how they would feel or perceive the situation. The ability to see the other person's perspective diminishes the feeling of being a victim and enhances compassion.

Letting go of being a victim of one's parents does not mean an individual has to like his parents or condone what they did to him. It does not mean approving of their behavior or letting the parents get away with mistreatment. It simply means he is no longer using his parents' behaviors to justify remaining dissatisfied, angry, helpless, or to justify difficulties or failures in his dealings with others.

Beware of Certain Traps

Real transformation requires not only an intellectual understanding but a corresponding emotional release or "connection" with the past, resulting in insight.

Crying, expressions of anger, and other forms of emotional release will not have long-lasting benefit unless a connection is made with how past self-limiting beliefs and grievances (often deeply repressed) are being maintained and then replayed in current situations.

Some people use insight to torture themselves. They take self-knowledge as indications of failure or forms of criticism and use it to convince themselves that they are defective and unworthy. Caterers need to observe themselves in a non-judgmental manner and not beat up on themselves every time they fall into a familiar emotional stew. Change cannot be forced, nor is there a report card for progress. Transformation takes place gradually over time and has its ups and down.

Some people become obsessed with their recovery and make it an all-consuming project. They take every workshop and seminar that comes along to prove how much they want to change. They talk the language of change and appear to be involved with growth, when, in fact, no actual changes have occurred. Others get on a soapbox to recruit everyone over to recovery but bypass their own inner work. A desperate quest for transformation often disguises an underlying resistance to change, as well as a preoccupation with performance and looking good.

In order to incur more self-disapproval, you also can judge others as being further along in their growth than you are. (Growth is often assessed very subjectively.) Or you can resent those who appear to be making good progress (again an subjective assessment) because you are unconsciously using the idea of their progress to feel inadequate by comparison.

Many people have a fantasy that transformation should result in some kind of permanent blissful state in which all problems and issues are eradicated. They think that recovery or inner peace means no more problems, no more emotional upsets. This notion of health is unrealistic.

All life is challenge and reaction. Each challenge in life should be different and unique and bring forth a spontaneous, creative reaction. This is how we grow. Problems, annoyances, or nuisances will always be encountered. The problem for most people is that they respond to problems inappropriately. They do not respond to what is happening in the moment so much as they respond to beliefs and perceptions acquired in their past.

A healthy person is able to handle disappointments and nuisances with minimal emotional stress. Often, she finds creative ways to turn the distress into something positive. Health does not mean never having a negative emotion, nor does it mean walking around with a blissful smile on one's face. Actually, as a person transforms, she may feel emotions more intensely than ever before and, at times, may feel more uncomfortable.

Some people experience catering withdrawal symptoms while in the process of letting go of catering behavior. Since catering gives a person a sense of identity, the caterer in the midst of growth may begin to

239

wonder, "Who am I? Can I really be myself? Will I like the new me?" One caterer expressed her transformation in these words, "Since I am no longer involved in helping others, I feel helpless, less in control, not needed, even worthless. There is no one to take care of anymore. I'm still looking for someone to take care of. I don't know who I am right now."

Fortunately, this emotional condition is only temporary and is gradually replaced by a new identity—a firm connection to one's genuine self—that is accompanied by new confidence.

It is a Western notion that in order to change ourselves, we must undertake some form of external activity. But behavioral modifications do not necessarily affect our inner being or change the degree of inner tension. Transformation of emotional catering requires inner realization of how we unconsciously look for deprivation and denigration and how we are conditioned to create these experiences.

Letting go of the attachments to being an innocent victim of someone else's malice or negligence produces a shift in the way we see things. This shift only occurs when an individual takes full responsibility for his feelings and circumstances.

When the shift occurs, positive changes automatically happen. You take charge of your life with ease and instinctively know what is best for you. You become less reactive, less angry, more detached, and better able to accept differences in others. Moderation and balance develop between protecting and caring for your own self-interests and giving and taking care of others. With minimal effort, you choose to create positive life scenarios. When you change your perspective on the world and others, everyone else appears to have changed.

A healthy person does not wait to get permission from others or from society to be what he wants. He is not afraid to be himself and express who he is. He gives himself permission to be all that he can be. To take that kind of personal power, you need to believe in yourself and take full responsibility for your life.

The Emotionally Independent Person

No one can predict all the benefits that will come to those who undertake to transform their patterns of emotional catering. But here is an indication of what life is like without the interference of a catering mentality.

Stacy, a 35-year-old teacher, described the progress she made in transforming her catering behavior: "I'm not angry anymore. I am able to see more clearly into other people's motives. I now realize that their negative behavior is a product of their own self-defeating perceptions. I no longer take their actions personally or assume they don't like me. Their actions say more about them and have little to do with me.

"I used to get so worried about others liking me. It's still nice to be liked, but I have no more thoughts or feelings about whether I am approved of. I rarely have any negative thoughts about myself.

"Even though my husband is still the same person, his traits no longer present a problem to me. I don't hurt because of who he is. I see him differently and I am beginning to love him in a completely new way.

"It's still scary to accept the wonderful positive changes that have occurred in my life. I used to be blocked emotionally, hard, sarcastic, and critical of everyone. Now I am able to reveal my true feelings and admit my mistakes. I have the ability to be honest and open with those closest to me. I feel compassion for others because I know we are all struggling with the same underlying issues of feeling hurt and unloved.

"I am more silent within myself. It's like a neutral feeling inside. There are times when I actually experience a kind of inner smile. I have my life back and I have a best friend—myself."

The emotionally independent person does not rely on external circumstances to feel good about herself. She no longer needs to be recognized or praised. Consequently, she gets more recognition and praise from others. She is not concerned whether others accept her or reject her, nor does she react defensively when others try to dominate or control her. She maintains her own integrity and is able to assert her rights and feelings appropriately without causing alienation from others. Injustices bounce off her. She is able to make the best out of challenging, difficult situations.

An emotionally independent person owns up to her faults and mistakes, without self-condemnation. Her words and actions are no longer split (say one thing but do another). Her life is a reflection of what she believes.

Being emotionally free, the person now has the capacity to sustain permanent loving relationships with others. She is not afraid of commitment, nor does she use her partner's weaknesses to feel disappointed, deprived, or neglected. she attracts into her life caring people who she formerly failed to consider and who treat her with honor and respect. She is able to express affection and caring directly to her immediate family members (not just strangers) without fear and on an everyday basis (not just sporadically).

The ability to generate love and express that love to those close to you is, in my view, the ultimate test of health and emotional freedom. This means that you are able to accept your immediate family and not judge them or want them to be the way you think they should be. Family members feel free to disagree with one another without hostility. They are curious about the other person's point of view rather than needing validation for their own position.

The person who is emotionally independent has no drive to change or save others or make them conform to her wishes. There is less concern with the inadequacies of others and fewer judgments to make. There is no need to please others or be what they want her to be. She is no longer pulled in by the "guilt-trips" of others. Her giving and caring have no secret motives.

A feeling of gratitude for what she has grows and deepens. She develops a trust in a positive future because change no longer represents loss; it feels like gain. She takes life as it comes in the present moment, while being prepared for the future. Life becomes stimulating, interesting, and fun, and her work becomes more creative and productive.

Many people will react to this description of health as impossible or unrealistic. It is true it will not happen overnight. But your belief it is not possible will block it from happening to you. The more we believe we are doomed to a life of deprivation and dissatisfaction, the more we make this our reality. If mental health cannot even be imagined, then there is little chance of it happening. The question is, can we really accept that much acknowledgment, self-respect, and inner satisfaction into our life? Can we let go of the frustrations and daily grievances that we have come to associate with being who we are and being alive? One of my clients made the following remark about inner growth: "It's really scary to me to face the possibility of attaining the success and satisfaction I've always believed would never happen."

Inner harmony does not mean withdrawal from the world. Actually, inner harmony expresses itself in a deepening interest and caring about others and the world. Inner harmony or peace is an energy, an aliveness in the body. This aliveness appears when there is no longer any conflict, guilt, or fear in the body. The feeling of "getting" or contentment comes from inside us, through our body. Our body is the source of intuition and pleasure. As one caterer noted, "I can't absorb pleasure. My body is like a rock. Praise and positive feedback bounce off me."

Healthy feelings and attributes cannot be consciously willed, forced, or pretended. They can only be obtained through a process of humbling self-observation. Don Juan, the Indian medicine man of Carlos Castaneda's books, said, "Self-importance is our greatest enemy. Think about it—what weakens us is feeling offended by the deeds and misdeeds of our fellow man. Our self-importance requires that we spend most of our time offended by someone."

When self-importance falls away, and we stop taking ourselves so seriously, every day offers possibilities of new and interesting sensations, amusements, and interactions. This is the experience of fun and play. Like a young child or a splashing dolphin, we can find life stimulating and exciting just in the pleasure of being alive. This is the nature of spirituality, a quality that is not pretended or performed and which comes from within.

Steeped in detached curiosity and humor, an individual begins to understand that life is not out there like a parent, giving to her only when she is good. Life does not judge her special because she has obeyed the rules and lived in conjunction with the norms of society. Nor does life judge her of no redeeming consequence if she does not win the gold medal for perfection. Life wants her highest good; it wants her to be happy and fulfilled. Personal happiness and contentment are there for the person who dares to cross the frontier of her own fears and opens her heart to receive the gifts the universe is waiting to bestow.

An individual can control the amount of pleasure, energy, and freedom that she feels. For most people, happiness and pleasure take some getting used to. Initially, our body cannot handle too high a voltage of pleasure, especially when our body has spent so many years attuned to misery. As the individual grows, pleasure and rejoicing are introduced in comfortable doses. Love, insight, and humor become antidotes to the programmed campaign of misery.

When people stop wasting time, energy, and money in creating an ideal image, they come to know and feel a deep reverence for life and a connection to all its forms, including other human beings, as well as animals and plants. They develop a deep inner compassion for all life. They understand that meaning comes from right living and through lasting and mutually satisfying relationships with those close to them.

The more you can accept what is and feel satisfied that you have enough, the more serene you can become. Consequently, joy and gratitude are able to permeate your life. Slowly you transform into a unique expression of the flowering of nature. In this flowering alone is the wonderful gift of getting. You do not want for anything, for you already are everything you need.

Appendix A

Exercises

The following exercises can be used on their own or as an adjunct to psychotherapy. They are designed to help you gain insight into your feelings and to facilitate taking responsibility for your own emotional reactions and stressful situations.

How to Work Through an Emotional Issue

This exercise can be used to work out emotional reactions, conflict with others, or grievances you are holding onto concerning people in your past or present.

- Describe what you perceived to have happened and define your emotional reaction. How did the situation make you feel? Go beneath the surface emotion, such as anger, fear, or sadness and describe what you felt was done to you. For example, "I'm furious because he betrayed me; he showed no consideration for my feelings. I felt tossed aside like an old rag doll." Or, "I felt terrified because I thought he would dump me, and leave me all alone." (Refer to Appendix B for help in defining feelings.)

- Take this feeling back into your past and describe similar feelings in your childhood. For example, "I remember feeling criticized a lot by my father. One time when I washed the floor for him, he criticized me for not doing the job well enough and told me I was useless." Or, "Mom always threatened to send me away to boarding school if I didn't do what she wanted." Feel and remember the original hurt.

- Recall how you have experienced those same

feelings at different times. Are these feelings a theme in your life? For example, "Yes, I've felt betrayed and rejected a lot. I felt betrayed by my boss and coworkers." Elaborate on those experiences.

- Do you look for betrayal and rejection even when they are not actually happening? Do you anticipate these feelings? Acknowledge the extent to which you hold onto feelings of betrayal and rejection.
- How do you provoke others so that you can experience these feelings? How do you collude in creating a problem? For example, "I could have paid more attention to my husband and what was going on between us. I needed to communicate my feelings directly to him rather than keeping them in and resenting him."
- Even if the other person did actually hurt you, you can either choose to feast on the hurt or let it go. Also, consider the situation from the other person's perspective. Once you disengage from feeling the victim, you will automatically find clarity and a more objective solution to your problem.
- Think of times when you may have betrayed others or treated them with a lack of consideration. There may be many times when you unwittingly subjected others to the same treatment you received.
- Describe how you treat yourself in the same manner. How do you betray yourself or treat yourself with a lack of consideration?

Wound Collecting

Make a list of past wounds or grievances with others. Describe how you were hurt. Explain how you expect or imagine that you will be hurt by others. Consider how you hold onto these hurts. Say to yourself, "I am choosing to hold onto this hurt."

For one week, write down in a notebook every time you experience a slight, a criticism, or a hurt from someone else. See how many wounds you collect. Avoid attempts to justify your right to feel hurt. Watch your tendency to jump onto hurts and indulge in them.

Understanding Illness

If you are experiencing significant illness or pains such as headaches, stomach troubles, muscle tension, etc., respond to the following instructions:

1. Describe in detail how your pain or illness makes you feel. For example, "My stiff neck makes me feel as if I'm being choked, strangled, burdened."

2. Visualize a form or an image for the pain or illness. For example, a dead weight across your shoulders, a noose around your neck, a fire in your throat, a boa constrictor squeezing the life out of you. Does the image have a color?

3. Imagine what the image would say if it spoke to you. Example, "I represent all the responsibility you are carrying around." Or, "I'm here to hold you back and keep you from attaining your goals."

4. What does the image remind you of? What parent or person evokes the same feelings? Physical pain can be a reaction to your emotional problems with a person or situation. Feelings of being controlled and rendered powerless can be recreated with pain or illness.

5. Does your illness enable you to avoid work or some project, get you attention, provide an excuse to fail in your life, or to remain dependent on others?

Childhood Regression

The purpose of this exercise is to understand how

hurtful feelings or grievances from childhood are transferred onto present relationships or events.

1. Focus on how you are feeling in your life right now, how you feel about yourself, what you are doing, and how you are relating to others. Describe your major emotional reactions.

2. Recall how you felt about yourself in your early years (pick a time). What was happening and how did you feel? How do those feelings compare with the present?

3. Go back further and see yourself as a child (pick an age). Let your mind wander to some hurtful or disturbing childhood event. See yourself as that child and experience the feelings associated with that event. How did you feel and how did you react? How did you defend or protect yourself? Reassure yourself that this experience is over.

4. Come back to the present and ask yourself how those old feelings affect your attitude toward life and other people? In what ways do you transfer those feelings onto people or circumstances in the present?

5. Describe how you may treat others or yourself in the manner you felt treated by your family members.

Appendix B

How to Define Your Feelings

Most people are unaware of their primary feelings. The following structure helps readers to contact primary feelings and to understand the difference between primary and secondary feelings. For the most part, primary feelings are unconscious and not experienced directly. They are often revealed by symbols, dreams, images, slips of the tongue, behaviors, or in psychotherapy.

Common Surface Behaviors or Symptoms:

Worry, sarcasm, overeating, no appetite, overworking, compulsive ambition, restlessness, anxiety, depression, apathy, boredom, irritation, insomnia, chronic fatigue, alcohol or drug abuse, impatience, psychosomatic ills, unrealistic optimism, heightened sense of responsibility, submissiveness, and self-pity. These feelings and behaviors mask the following secondary feelings.

Secondary Feelings or Defenses (Can be Conscious or Unconscious):

Frustration, anger, rage, despair, sadness, fear, dread, loss, loneliness; self-reproach or feelings of inadequacy; feelings of being bad, stupid, guilty, or shameful; impulses to blame others and to retaliate; emotional impotency, avoidance of others, numbness.

These feelings and reactions cover up our indulgence in the following primary feelings. This is the deeper level we really want to understand. Our painful surface symptoms and self-defeating behaviors originate from our unconscious attachments to the following negative emotions.

Primary Feelings (unconscious)—three major categories:

1. *Oral Feelings:* expectations of loss, starving and going without, feeling held up, having to wait, being deprived of what you really want, missing out, never having enough or feeling satisfied, drained ("they take everything from me, I get nothing"); feeling refused, denied, not given to, disappointed, helpless, suffocated, devoured; watching others get away with things, seeing others excel and feeling less, feeling there is nothing here for you.

2. *Control Feelings:* feeling taken advantage of, used, squashed, screwed, ripped off, conned, violated, tricked, lied to, persecuted, intimidated, trapped, pushed around, forced to submit, dominated, overpowered,

passive, imposed upon; having to endure inappropriate behavior from others; giving up your own perceptions and beliefs to others.

3. *Rejection Feelings:* feeling abandoned, insignificant, neglected, not wanted, excluded, looked down upon as no good, put down, criticized, unfairly accused, not understood, not liked, hated, not acknowledged or recognized, not taken seriously, unappreciated, dismissed, ignored, unworthy, not supported, not validated; unable to depend on anyone, let down, betrayed, made a fool of, scolded, discredited, ridiculed, condemned.

Appendix C

Emotional Catering Inventory

The following statements reflect catering behaviors. Consider each statement carefully and, as sincerely as you can, answer *yes* or *no.* (Many caterers are in denial and cannot see themselves objectively. Their responses to these statements might not reflect their true state of mind.)

1. I am easily swayed and influenced by the opinions and attitudes of others. Yes No
2. I tend to go along with the decisions and wishes of others rather than assert my own. Y N
3. I have a need to look good and appear to others as though I have no problems. Y N
4. I avoid stating my views and opinions, particularly if I suspect they are not shared by others. Y N
5. I am concerned with making other people happy regardless of my own feelings and needs. Y N
6. I usually turn to mush and get anxious when others are angry with me. Y N

7. When others are angry or upset, I try to calm them down and smooth things over. Y (N)

8. It is very hard for me to take criticism. Y (N)

9. I find myself at times to be critical and judgmental of others. (Y) N

10. I have a tendency to blame others or situations for my own failures and bad moods. (Y) N

11. When challenged, I usually become defensive and offer explanations and excuses for my behavior. Y (N)

12. I compare myself a lot with others and feel either inferior or superior. (Y) N

13. I have difficulty expressing and asserting my needs to others. Y (N)

14. I tend to express my anger inappropriately. (Y) N

15. I have a problem saying "no" to others without feeling guilty and selfish. Y (N)

16. I tend to apologize for my behavior, even when I am not at fault. Y (N)

17. I find myself wanting to change others to fit my expectations and needs. (Y) N

18. I usually insist on getting my own way. Y (N)

19. I am not sure of what I want in life. (Y) N

20. I have difficulty pursuing my goals and following through to a constructive end. (Y) N

21. I have problems making decisions. (Y) N

22. I need the validation and approval of others to feel good about myself. Y (N)

23. It is hard for me to look squarely at my own faults and own up to my mistakes. (Y) N

24. I feel that a lot of what happens is my fault. Y (N)

25. I judge myself harshly and rarely feel I handle things well enough. (Y) N

26. I tend to avoid my problems, pretend they do not exist, or wait and hope they go away. Y (N)

27. I dwell on possible calamities. (Y) N

28. I find it difficult to get close to others. Y (N)

29. I do not seem to attract people who treat me with honor and respect. Y (N)
30. I withhold my innermost thoughts and feelings from the one I am romantically involved with. Y (N)
31. I feel the need to rescue others and cure them of their weaknesses. Y (N)
32. I feel a victim of the faults and weaknesses of others. Y (N)
33. It is difficult for me to express affection and love to others. Y (N)
34. I do not expect that my feelings, opinions, and views will be heard. Y (N)
35. I feel uncomfortable or embarrassed when I am praised. Y (N)
36. I have a problem getting out of situations or relationships that are destructive. Y (N)
37. I focus more on the problems of others than on my own feelings. Y (N)
38. Most of the time I feel that others are more powerful and intelligent than I am. Y (N)
39. I tend to reveal too much of myself to others, often to my own disadvantage. Y (N)
40. I inwardly feel superior, special, unique, or different from others. (Y) N
41. I need to have the important people in my life agree with me and believe the way I do. Y (N)
42. I endure unpleasant situations rather than take constructive action. Y (N)
43. I focus on and draw attention to my mistakes and inadequacies. (Y) N
44. I am preoccupied with personal achievement and being seen as perfect. (Y) N
45. I tend to hold grudges against those who slight me. (Y) N
46. I often feel that others get more than I do. (Y) N
47. I worry excessively and do not trust that things will

253

work out positively for me. (Y) N

48. I frequently feel bored. (Y) N
49. I feel insecure, guilty, and obligated when someone gives to me. Y (N)
50. I tend to take on too much responsibility in my work and in my relationships. (Y) N
51. I feel that others will reject me if they knew the real me. Y (N)
52. Much of the time I feel that I cannot do anything right. Y (N)
53. I feel I do not deserve good things and happiness in my life. Y (N)
54. I sometimes feel I am the only person who can do things right. (Y) N
55. I often feel controlled by outside events and other people. (Y) N
56. I fear losing those I love or what I have. (Y) N
57. I often feel that others are not there for me when I need them. Y (N)
58. I expect my relationships to provide me with all my good feelings. Y (N)
59. I try to say what I think will please others. Y (N)
60. I sometimes lie to protect myself. Y (N)
61. I feel I cannot trust others or rely on them for support or to get things done. (Y) N
62. I have a hard time relaxing, having fun, and being spontaneous. Y (N)

Total your *yes* answers: 25 The higher your score, the greater your emotional-catering tendencies.

Appendix D

Anatomy of the Emotional Catering Structure

This is another approach to understanding our feelings, as presented in Appendix B.

Surface behaviors and emotions:

The caterer: bends over backwards to serve others; goes along with the agenda of others; rescues, pleases, handles everything; compulsively needs to show care and attention to others; worries about the approval of others; strives to excel.

The above behaviors and emotions are reactions to the following emotional difficulties:

Feeling guilt about hurting or offending others; considering oneself as inadequate, inconsiderate, selfish, and self-centered; feeling guilt over letting others down and self-reproach at not being able to satisfy others; feelings of wanting to refuse others and have nothing to do with them; anger at *not getting*; fantasies of hurting others; numbness and I-don't- care attitude; fantasies of running away.

Beneath these emotional difficulties, the caterer is unconsciously attached to:

a) feelings of having to submit and perform for others at great cost to oneself;

b) not getting emotional nourishment or acknowledgment for one's efforts;

c) being denied and neglected, having one's desires and needs discouraged and not allowed;

d) feeling controlled, restrained, and forced to give up one's opinions and feelings and submit to someone else's program;

e) feeling looked down upon by others as inadequate,

inferior, and having no redeeming value;

f) feeling rejected, ignored, betrayed, abandoned, and unloved.

Appendix E

While children can see the world with an open sense of wonder, they also have self-centered ways of perceiving reality. The following features describe some of these self-centered perceptions. These childish patterns of perception persist into our adult years, causing emotional turmoil within us and in our relationships. Notice that in each of these features a comparison is made between the child's way of interpreting reality and that of the emotionally independent person.

1. Immediate Gratification with no Effort

The child wants instant gratification and does not want to work for it. He resents being made to expend effort. Much of our advertising and consumerism is based on this desire for instant gratification. Many overweight adults want to lose weight immediately but do not want to give up their eating pleasures or strive for good health. Young adults want to be professionals and earn lots of money, but do not want to expend the effort to reach the goal.

Emotionally independent people are able to delay the satisfaction of achieving goals. They realize that mastery of any skill or talent takes time and effort, and they do not feel deprived by the lengthy process of accomplishment.

2. "Everyone Is Looking at Me and Judging Me"

Children believe the whole world is preoccupied with them. Many adults feel the same way. As one woman put it, "I know the people in the restaurant are watching me eat and judging what I put in my mouth." Many adults are convinced that everyone is eyeing them with critical judgment at social gatherings or parties.

The emotionally independent person is not concerned with how others see her. She has worked through her self-importance and understands emotionally as well as intellectually that she is not the center of the universe. She knows that most people are more concerned with themselves than with others.

3. Cause and Effect: "I Make Everything Happen"

Children believe they cause things to happen or cause others to be upset. They believe if something goes wrong, they are to blame. Conversely, they also blame others or substances for their actions, "He made me do it."

Adults, as well, have a hard time owning up to their inappropriate behavior. They believe, "The devil (or alcohol) made me do it," or "The movie caused me to act that way." They also claim power over the emotional reactions of others: "He would not have gotten angry if I had remained silent." Many adults also believe their actions cause bad things to happen: "The hurricane destroyed our house because we sinned." Feelings of guilt and retribution are linked to the child's notion of cause and effect.

The emotionally independent person takes responsibility for herself and understands that she "co-creates" her experience. She understands that on some level she chooses how she interacts with her environment. She does not claim power over the capriciousness of events.

4. Magical Thinking

Children believe that the sun comes out to make them happy and that the moon follows them on walks. They are not yet able to differentiate between the internal world and the external universe. Children believe they have a special relationship with fate.

In adults, magical thinking often takes the form of signs: "If we don't sell our house, it's a sign we shouldn't move." Or, "This good-luck charm will save me from harm." The gambler says, "The sun is out; therefore, I'm going to win."

Emotionally independent people accept fate as random and do not personalize what happens to them. They understand they cannot control everything that happens in their lives.

5. Win-Lose

Children see the world as black or white, good or bad, win or lose: "If I get, others lose; if others get, I lose; if I submit, Daddy wins; if people don't agree with me, they are against me; if Susie's good, I'm bad."

Caterers are also steeped in an either-or, win-lose mentality: "If I don't win first place, I'm no good; if Sally is beautiful, I'm ugly; if I give in to my husband, I lose."

The emotionally independent person does not see the world as either-or, positive or negative. She accepts the existence of the negative as well as the positive and can see shades of gray. She believes in win-win and is open to differing perspectives. There is no feeling of being one up or one down.

6. "Everyone Sees Things the Way I Do"

Children believe their way of seeing things is the only way. Being extremely self-centered, they are unable to see from different perspectives. Many adults also assume that others see events the way they do, and are surprised to discover that their partners or their children have a completely different viewpoint from their own.

The emotionally independent person realizes that everyone has her own unique way of perceiving reality. She believes in the peaceful co-existence of differing mentalities. She is open to new perspectives and opinions and not afraid to change her views when new ideas are presented.

7. This Will Never End

When children experience something unpleasant, it

feels as though the feeling will go on forever. They believe things will never change or improve. For example, they say, "I'll never get that ice cream cone." Adults can also see no end in sight when they are caught up in an emotional morass: "I'll be depressed forever; nothing will work out for me; things will never change."

For the emotionally independent person, however, life changes. Their motto: "And this too shall pass." Each day presents new opportunities for happiness or betterment.

8. Never Gets Enough and Doesn't Want to Share

Children believe that everything is theirs or should be. They resent sharing and feel deprived if they have to give. In their minds, there is only one cookie. If they don't get it, they will be deprived forever. The child focuses on the toy or ice-cream cone he didn't get. If he sees another child playing with a toy, he wants it. He is steeped in feelings of unfairness. Others, he believes, always get more.

Adults, as well, can feel deprived if they are asked to give or share. They can feel just as possessive with their belongings and dissatisfied with their possessions. They peep at others who seem to have more and feel shortchanged.

The emotionally independent person knows there is plenty to go around, and she trusts that she will have her fill. She understands that love has no limits. She feels gratitude for what she has and a sense of appreciation for life.

9. "I'm the Only One Who Feels this Way"

Children believe that their experiences are unique and that no one else has similar feelings. Thus, they often feel misunderstood and alone. Adults, too, are prone to feel misunderstood and are often surprised when they discover that others have the same feelings they do.

Emotionally independent people understand that at an emotional level we are very much alike; we share the

259

same feelings and experiences. Consequently, they rarely feel misunderstood. They are able to show compassion when others express negative emotions because they have experienced the same emotions.

10. Makes Bold Assertions without Facts

A child makes bold statements about reality without regard for the facts. His egocentricity does not allow him to differentiate between his point of view and that of others. This same aspect appears in adults. For example, a man asserts, "My wife never gives me what I want." When asked to give an example, he fails to substantiate his complaint. He just "knows" she is withholding.

The emotionally independent person, however, refrains from making statements or assertions that cannot be followed up with specific examples.

Bibliography

Bergler, Edmund, M.D., *Tensions Can Be Reduced to Nuisances,* Liveright Publishing Co., Liveright Paperback Edition, 1978, New York.

Bergler, Edmund, M.D. *Curable and Incurable Neurotics,* Liveright Publishing Co., New York, 1961. p. 25.

Branden, Nathaniel, *Honoring the Self,* Jeremy P. Tarcher, Inc., Los Angeles, 1983, pg. 116.

Castaneda, Carlos, *The Fire from Within,* Pocket Books, Division of Simon & Schuster, Inc., New York, 1984. p. 2.

Elkind, David, *Child Development and Education: A Piagetian Perspective,* Oxford University Press, New York, 1976.

Klein, Melanie, *The Psychology of Children,* London, 1934.

Kramer, Joel, *The Passionate Mind,* North Atlantic Books, Berkeley, Calif. 1974, 1983.

Miller, Alice, *For Your Own Good,* Farrar, Straus, Giroux, New York, 1983.

Richmond, P.G., *An Introduction to Piaget,* Basic Books Inc., New York, 1971.

Roheim, Geza, *Psychoanalysis and Anthropology,* International Universities Press, New York, 1950.

Sandra Michaelson (1944-1999) was a psychotherapist in private practice from 1979 to 1999. She owned and directed the Naples New Life Counseling Center in Naples, Florida, for eight years. Sandra has had many years of training in Gestalt, Psychosynthesis, Primal, and Cognitive therapies. From 1985, she was involved in an innovative therapeutic process known as Berglerian Analysis, a method based on the work of Edmund Bergler (1900-1962). This method recognizes and neutralizes unconscious self-defeating patterns, producing new insight, creativity, and inner peace. She was one of the few practitioners in the United States using this highly effective method. Sandra conducted numerous groups and seminars and gave many lectures. She specialized in issues of codependency, self-esteem, creativity, depression, and addictive disorders. Along with her practice, she trained other therapists in this method. She is the author of two other psychology books, both dealing with relationship issues.

She moved from Florida to Santa Fe, N.M., in 1993 and continued her work there until her death from breast cancer in 1999. Her work is carried on and made available by her husband, Peter Michaelson, at his depth psychology website, **www.WhyWeSuffer.com**.

Made in the
USA
Middletown, DE